Beyond Silence

WITHDRAWN

Also by Daniel Hoffman

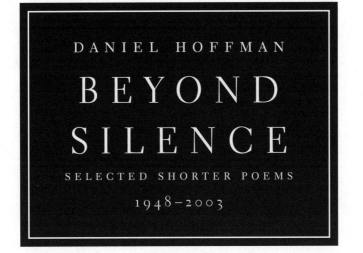

DANIEL HOFFMAN

BEYOND SILENCE

SELECTED SHORTER POEMS

1948–2003

Then inward darkness burns away,
Shards of silence frame the essential psalm.

LOUISIANA STATE UNIVERSITY PRESS

BATON ROUGE

2003

cloth
12   11   10   09   08   07   06   05   04   03
5   4   3   2   1
paper
12   11   10   09   08   07   06   05   04   03
5   4   3   2   1

Designer: Melanie O'Quinn Samaha
Typeface: Bembo
Typesetter: Coghill Composition Co., Inc.
Printer and binder: Thomson-Shore, Inc.

Library of Congress Cataloging-in-Publication Data

Hoffman, Daniel, 1923–
    Beyond silence : selected shorter poems, 1948–2003 / Daniel Hoffman.
        p.   cm.
    ISBN 0-8071-2860-0 (alk. paper) — ISBN 0-8071-2861-9 (pbk. : alk. paper)
    I. Title.

PS3515.O2416 B49   2003
811'.54—dc21   2002034090

Publication of this book has been supported by a
grant from the National Endowment for the Arts
in Washington, D.C., a federal agency.

NATIONAL
ENDOWMENT
FOR THE ARTS

For E. McF. H.

What is an island without the sea?

Contents

IV

V

VI

VII

VIII

Preface

This volume includes poems chosen from my previous seven books of verse: *An Armada of Thirty Whales* (1954), *A Little Geste* (1960), *The City of Satisfactions* (1963), *Striking the Stones* (1968), *The Center of Attention* (1974), *Hang-Gliding from Helicon* (1988), and *Darkening Water* (2002). The original publication of poems is indicated at the foot of the page; those without book titles present new poems. I have excluded longer poems and most sonnets, to be gathered in future collections, nor have I excerpted from my two book-length poems—*Middens of the Tribe,* a novel in verse, and *Brotherly Love,* a historical meditation of William Penn's treaty with the Indians and the founding of Pennsylvania.

The poems in this book are arranged thematically, not chronologically. I seem to have written perhaps too abundantly, and can but trust that each poem be different from the others. My hope is that they will each give pleasure.

Poems appearing in book form for the first time here were originally published in *Literary Imagination:* "Poe's Tomb"; and the *Philadelphia Inquirer:* "Owed to Dejection."

The Poem

Arriving at last

It has stumbled across the harsh
Stones, the black marshes.

True to itself, by what craft
And strength it has, it has come
As a sole survivor returns

From the steep pass.
Carved on memory's staff
The legend is nearly decipherable.
It has lived up to its vows

If it endures
The journey through the dark places
To bear witness,
Casting its message
In a sort of singing.

[Hang-Gliding from Helicon]

1

I

In the Days of Rin-Tin-Tin

In the days of Rin-Tin-Tin
There was no such thing as sin,
No boymade mischief worth God's wrath
And the good dog dogged the badman's path.

In the nights, the deliquescent horn of Bix
Gave presentiments of the pleasures of sex;
In the Ostrich Walk we walked by twos—
Ja-da, jing-jing, what could we lose?

The Elders mastered The Market, Mah-jongg,
Readily admitted the Victorians wrong,
While Caligari hobbled with his stick and his ghoul
And overtook the Little Fellow on his way to school.

[A Little Geste]

5

The Twentieth Century

A squad of soldiers lies beside a river.
They're in China—see the brimmed gables piled
On the pagoda. The rows of trees are lopped
And the Chinese soldiers have been stopped
In their tracks. Their bodies lie
In bodily postures of the dead,

Arms bound, legs akimbo and askew,
But look how independently their heads
Lie thereabouts, some upright, some of the heads
Tipped on their sides, or standing on their heads.
Mostly, the eyes are open
And their mouths twisted in a sort of smile.

Some seem to be saying or just to have said
Some message in Chinese just as the blade
Nicked the sunlight and the head dropped
Like a sliced cantaloupe to the ground, the cropped
Body twisting from the execution block.
And see, there kneels the executioner

Wiping his scimitar upon a torso's ripped
Sash. At ease, the victors smoke. A gash
Of throats darkens the riverbed. 1900. The Boxer
Rebellion. Everyone there is dead now.
What was it those unbodied mouths were saying?
A million arteries stain the Yellow River.

[The Center of Attention]

6

Flushing Meadows, 1939

Lightning! Lightning! Lightning! Without thunder!
A zaggedy white trombone of lightshot, crackling
Between metallic globules, egglike, hugely
Aching in the corners of our eyes—
The afterburn of electrocuted air
Sizzled into our ears and nostrils, halfblinded
Us. We reeled into the dim sunshine
Groping a little, holding hands, still hearing
The confident vibrant voice of the sound system—
"Harnessed . . . power . . . unnumbered benefits . . ."
And this we pondered down the bedecked Concourse
Of Nations. A gold-robed King of Poland brandished
Crossed swords on horseback pedestalled on high;
The Soviet Citizen bore his sanguine star
Almost as high as that American flag
That snaffled in the smart wind perched atop
The Amusement Park's live parachute drop.
Trapped in antique mores, now the sun
Abandoned the International Pavilions
To miracles of manmade light. The trees
In their pots were underlit, revealing pasty
Backsides of their embarrassed leaves. We barked
The shins of our puppylove against the crowds
That swirled around us, swirled like fallen leaves
In the wind's vortex toward the Pool of Fountains:
Mauve and yellowing geysers surged and fell
As national anthems tolled, amity-wise,
From the State of Florida's Spanish Carillon.
What portent, in that luminous night to share
Undyingly, discovery of each other!
Helen, Helen, thy beauty is to me
Like those immutable emblems, huge and pure—
One glimmering globe the world's will unifying
Beside spired hope that ravels the deep skies,
Our time's unnumbered benefits descrying
In their own light's shimmer, though the new dawn comes
With lightning, lightening in a murmur of summer thunder.

[A Little Geste]

7

The seals in Penobscot Bay

hadn't heard of the atom bomb,
so I shouted a warning to them.

Our destroyer (on trial run) slid by
the rocks where they gamboled and played;

they must have misunderstood,
or perhaps not one of them heard

me over the engines and tides.
As I watched them over our wake

I saw their sleek skins in the sun
ripple, light-flecked, on the rock,

plunge, bubbling, into the brine,
and couple & laugh in the troughs

between the waves' whitecaps and froth.
Then the males clambered clumsily up

and lustily crowed like seacocks,
sure that their prowess held thrall

all the sharks, other seals, and seagulls.
And daintily flipped the females,

seawenches with musical tails;
each looked at the Atlantic as

though it were her looking-glass.
If my warning had ever been heard

it was sound none would now ever heed.
And I, while I watched those far seals,

tasted honey that buzzed in my ears
and saw, out to windward, the sails

of an obsolete ship with banked oars
that swept like two combs through the spray

And I wished for a vacuum of wax
to ward away all those strange sounds,

yet I envied the sweet agony
of him who was tied to the mast,

when the boom, when the boom, when the boom
of guns punched dark holes in the sky.

[An Armada of Thirty Whales]

Blood

At a wolf's wild dugs
When the world was young
With eager tongue
Twin brothers tugged,

From foster mother
Drew their nurture.
Her harsh milk ran
Thence in the blood of man,

In the blood of kings
Who contrived the State.
What wolvish lust to lead the pack
The memory of that taste brings back.

[The Center of Attention]

10

The Battle of Hastings

Schoolboys in blazers infiltrate the aisles
Of the British Museum. It's hard to read
Maps of the Battle of Hastings
While their master futilely harangues them

About the Battle of Hastings. They are intent
On tactics of their own making.
A lot they care for the plight of Harold (his forces
Bloodied and wearied from besting the Norsemen

Hundreds of miles to the north ten days before),
The Fourth Form will maintain its hegemony
Over the Third this day, come what may! At last
Their skirmish deploys through doorways, advancing

Into the Hall of Clocks. Another battalion
In blazers—maroon, not green—troops through the Map Room
Scuffling, and out, save for one laggard, a toddler
But three feet tall. He can't even see into the cases.

His head is large, his legs and arms are stubby and bent,
His steps necessarily small. And now two boys
In green for some reason retrace their steps,
Sniffling. Down the center aisle, they catch a glimpse

Of maroon, the enemy color, and rush
To opposite sides of the hall. They have him
Cornered!—then see he's not a mere babe in Infants, but their age,
A midget-sized monster providentially provided

For their satisfaction. He watches the boy at one end
Of the aisle, sees the eyes gleam, the curled lip
Of one waiting for him to come nearer. He turns
And at the other end of the aisle, sees

The other, lip curled and eyes eager to torment him.
He suddenly ducks under the cases, bobs up in the next aisle
But they move over an aisle and are waiting as before.
He is trapped, there is no escaping

Being born to endure the revenge of unknown adversaries
For an offense of which he must be innocent
Except for being born. I saw the terror
In that boy's face, and the desperate resolve

To run, or if he couldn't, then to do
His poor best for honor's sake
And not go down snivelling beneath the blows
Of the always larger, stronger. This was one

Battle in a series already long that might
Be averted—*"Young man,"* I said, *"I'm lost—*
Perhaps you can show me the way out?"
And so let him lead me to safety

Through his enemies, as though there is
A way out. In the entrance hall, surprised
By what they see beside me, others turn
With heedless stare and curious intent;

He pretends he doesn't notice them.
I thank him. I must go. The lines
Are being drawn. Among the columns
He appraises his next defensive position.

[Hang-Gliding from Helicon]

A Special Train

Banners! Bunting! The engine throbs
In waves of heat, a stifling glare
Tinges the observation-car

And there, leaning over the railing
What am I
Doing in the Orient?

Blackflies, shrapnel-thick, make bullocks
Twitch. The peasants stand
Still as shrines,

And look, in this paddy
A little boy is putting in the shoots.
He's naked in the sunlight. It's my son!

There he is again, in that
Field where the earth-walls meet.
It's his play-time. See, his hands are smeared

With mud, and now his white
Back is flecked with ash, is seared
By embers dropping from the sky—

The train chuffs past. I cry
Stop! Stop! We cross another paddy.
He's there, he's fallen in the mud, he moans my name.

[Broken Laws]

Crop-Dusting

The mice rot in their tunnels in a field
Where phantom harvesters cut phantom grain.
A poisoned acre grows a poisoned yield.

Here skinny children stretch their hands in vain.
Their swollen bellies hurt, and are not healed.
A phantom blade has harvested their grain.

Night after night I see this land annealed
By draughts of fire and death that fall like rain.
One poisoned acre poisons all the field.

These are my crops. We harrow my domain.
The one who pays counts all for which he's billed.
A phantom harvester stacks phantom grain.

To own such wealth as this my heart I've steeled
And all but stilled the tumult in my brain.
My poisoned acre grows a poisoned yield.

Unable to be dispossessed by Cain,
In his accounts my civil tithes are sealed.
And how renounce the poisoning of this field,
Or be forgiven the reaping of its grain?

[Striking the Stones]

The Pursued

Surely he'd outwitted them, outdistanced them and earned
Respite at this café. There goes the ferry.
Two trips risked in his own person, over
And back, and now, in this wig
Crossed again. Nobody knew him.
Coffee under the arbor, mission done,
Content. And then he recognized
The first signs—
Heat, hotter than the day's heat, swarming
And his skin parched, stretching
Tight about each finger; the eyes
Pounding: arbor, harbor,
Table, gable, all begin to swing
Up and forth, forth and up, up and so, until
Giddily earth grinds beneath him, shudders;
Sweat oozes icy on his neck now,
On shaking chest a shirt of seaweed crawls,
Iron table rat-tat-tat-tat-tats against his elbow
Though harbor's calm and arbor's still. You've seen
A stepped-on centipede left on the pavement,
Each limb's oracular gesticulations?
—Cutting through the scent of pear trees
Klaxons, baying, toil up up the highroad,
Vans of his other pursuers.

[The City of Satisfactions]

15

The Victor

When the fight was over
And the enemy lay dead
The victor shuddered in a daze,
Holding the butchered head

Of one whose strength had all but matched his strength,
Whose wile he undid by his guile.
Proven, his own superiority.
Still he quakes, tasting in victory

Blood hated, yet prized.
He had put on
That murderous character, in foe despised,
And how suck air in innocence again?

[Striking the Stones]

Shaking the President's Hand

Who'd be likely to forget
His brief squeeze by those brisk fingers,
The First Citizen's! The touch of kings
Was blessed, a gift to remedy
The King's Evil. Here
Where every man's a king,
What did I touch a President to cure?

[Striking the Stones]

A Historian

The dead again
Burst from their levelled graves
They reassemble on the hill
Ready for disastrous victory
Where a great empire fell
On its foe and fell

Again in the hot wide
Landscape of his mind
The captains sit astride
Their festooned chomping horses send
Battalions into certain
Enfilade

O they can never
Change the outcome they have fought
This battle over
Never knowing
Why they are there
Still following

Tattered pennants ignorant
Of trade routes or the pride
Of prince or diplomat whose ruse
Charges them to ride
The bloodspecked foaming crest
Of this riptide

No more than he can know
The soldier's brute obedience to orders
The captain's fealty to the general's plan
The commanders wrapped in webbed illusion
That their strategy will follow
Their will

Nor know the iron taste of fear
In throats that do not seem a part
Of the same contraption as the legs
Wildly going their own way

Or the gut that retches at the smell of blood
Or the heart

Booming its dark cannonade
Until the heartbeat or the battle ends.
The tallying of losses starts again.
The sky thickens with buzzards' wings.
They settle, gorge, and circle, waiting for
The future

[Broken Laws]

In Memory of Lewis Corey

I

He knew I'd never be a true disciple
When I coughed, embarrassed by his love
For Swinburne. Then, I thought
A real reformer ought
To praise revolt in *everything*.
But he'd no use for verse that didn't "sing."
And so he taught
(I didn't know it for a lesson yet)
That poetry and politics
Don't mix
In simple rhetorics. You can see
How young I was, how out of fashion he.
I since have read of Fraina in a book,
How Madison Square Garden rose and shook
At his command, ten thousand voices one
Vowing to free
From imperialist invasion
Archangel far across the sea.
But what's all that to me?
I wasn't even born when Fraina led
His fractious splinter in those Red
Matchstick plays at power.
The man I honor is the man I knew:
Self-purged before the Moscow Trials,
He came through
The withering away, as at the stake,
Of every vow his fervent youth could make
But one, and that the most romantic trust
That shown the injustice of our institutions,
We will choose to make them just.

Corey had long done with revolutions,
But I confess, I haven't found mankind
As sensible as he to what enlightened mind
Describes as the common good
To a self-seeking multitude.
It's fifteen years he's dead now, yet the thought
Of Corey makes my mind rehearse

All that he taught,
And this thought chides—
How little else have I reformed, besides
The diction of my verse;
Should the commonwealth, like art, seek perfect forms
What can it learn from my self-searching trade?
Those were the images he made,
Those, and the image of a man possessed
By reason to persuade
A race spoon-fed upon self-interest
To set the table, break its hoarded bread.
What can I do with his bequest
Who wished no man to suffer wrong,
But make his memory a song?

II

It was a time that cowardice
Begat upon disgrace;
What else had numbed all decent sense
In so many in high place,
While those whom popular hatred fed
Rose up by being base?
       —As we may remember.

They tarred him with black printer's ink,
They smeared him in the town,
They bought a hireling liar
To cry his good name down.
But what can harm his spirit now?
He's gone to his renown,
       —As we may remember.

For he's an honored citizen
In the republic of the dead,
And we who were his countrymen
—Now let the truth be said—
May learn to cut our plenty's loaf
With his blessing on our bread.

[Broken Laws]

The Princess Casamassima

After digging in the rubble of the ruined house
For nine days
They've found a *third* corpse—
No fingerprints; no hands.
One leg and the head blown off.
The story in the *Times*
Didn't even tell
The sex of the torso . . .

These were some of the people
Who'd take power to the people
In their own hands.
All their questions have one answer.
Dynamite
Makes non-negotiable demands
For an apocalypse,
In case of survivors.

Once, another world ago,
There was a girl I never dreamed
Would be like them:
She seemed to lack nothing
—Looks, friends, certainly a silver
Spoon had stirred her porringer—
She'd sit scribbling
Notes in the next to the back row,

But I can't remember now
One word she wrote for me.
—Good God,
Was it something *I* said
About Thoreau
Shorted her fuse? Oh,
Such unbalanced, mad
Action is surely extra-curricular—

If the discourse of our liberal arts
Which entertains all rival truths as friends
And rival visions reconciles
Could but bring the pleasures of its wholeness

To a mind
Rent by frenzy—
But how conceive what hatred
Of the self, turned inside-out, reviles

The whole great beckoning world, or what desire
Sentenced the soul
To that dark cellar where all life became
So foul
With the pitch of rage,
Rage, rage, rage to set aflame
Father's house—what can assuage
That fire or that misfire?

[The Center of Attention]

23

Power

"My life is a one-billionth part
Of history. I wish I was dead."

He rips the page from his notebook.
Litter in a rented room.

The neighbors will barely remember
His silence when they said Hello.

They'll not forget his odd smile.
Nobody comes to see him.

When he thinks of his folks he smiles oddly.
"It was broken but was it a home?"

At night, the wet dream. Arising,
He is afraid of women.

In his notebook, "Power over people!"
His job, scouring pots in a hash-house.

At last he will pick up a girl.
She'll think, Does he ever need love—

But I don't like him at all.
Her Mom will hang up on his phone call.

One day he will fondle a snub-nosed
Pistol deep in his pants.

What is his aim? The TV,
Even bumper stickers remind him

Who has the face and the name
His name and smile will replace.

His trigger will make him bigger.
He will become his victim.

When he steps from his rented room
History is in his hand.

[The Center of Attention]

Violence

After I'd read my poem about a brawl
between two sidewalk hustlers—one,
insulted, throws the other down and nearly
kills him—over coffee and cookies a grave

senior citizen reproved me: *How
could you see such violence and you
didn't try to stop them?*—Oh, I explained,
it wasn't like that, really—I saw

two guys in a shoving match and thought
I'd write about aggression, what
anger really feels like. . . . *Yes,*

*and if the one got killed
it would be on your head.
You should've stopped them,* he said.

[Darkening Water]

Mean Street

In sneaks, in shorts, in tie-dyed tee-shirts,
one burly, blond, the other swarthy,
leaner, younger, snatch at each other
circling, till one gets an armlock
on the other's head. A pretty hot day for
fooling around with Greco-Roman,
or is it Catch-as-Catch-Can?—only
they're not fooling. They edge each other
grimly within the ring of onlookers
each trying to throw the other off
balance, enormous effort—the lean one
shoves his knee between the other's
legs and down they fall, hard
on the cracked pavement, scattering tattered
piles of magazines, the plastic
sunglasses with sequins or without,
each merchandise displayed on two
squares of pavement precisely, as though
by treaty, jumbled as the blond guy
lands on his back in grime, trying
to arch his back, to turn, but the lean one
prevents and pinions him, then grasps
a fistful of his long hair and beats
the back of his head on the pavement, a *thud*
and a *thud,* a *thud*—If y'ever call
me that again—a *thud*—I'll KILL ya,
d'ya hear? his flushed tiger face
glares, fangs bared. On his back
the blond guy looks scared, feebly
surrenders. He's had it. The insulted feels
the insult, whatever it was, was not
worth really killing the bastard
—though it feels good, good, the power
to do it, calm with surely knowing
a couple or three more *thuds*—so easy!—
and the guy'd be dead. So, can it
satisfy, letting him off with
just the pain, the fear, and then
remembering the fear, the pain?

Still holds his hair, could give a quick
yank, a real *thud* . . . But no,
he'll be content, this time, to gloat
on the other's fear, his pain, his shame.
They separate, get up, dust off,
the loser gazing far away,
the victor staring through him while
the passersby who'd stopped their passing
to form the ring that made this brawl
a gladiator's struggle break
and melt away. A couple stay
to help re-establish peace,
gathering the sunshades flung
or kicked into the gutter, stacking
the magazines in rows again.
Grimly, the merchants mind their wares.
They've made no sales. The people fade.
A taut, baneful silence reigns.

[Darkening Water]

A Sidewalk Scene

It's a *modus vivendi* of sorts, not dying
on a heap of rags and a dirty blanket, lying
beneath a plastic sheet and three umbrellas,
handles linked with string, their ribs a trellis
just above the head shielded from rain
while *sotto voce* carrying on again
half a dialogue, tracing in air
an impatient or expressive gesture,
now dropping filthy fingers from a face
wrinkled as the map of Iceland, toothless,
mumbling a reply to someone else
not there to hear her catalogue of ills
as back and forth she's rocking, back and forth,
back and forth, as one who by the hearth
holds an infant, or is an infant held.
The passers pass her by, their steps unstilled
by the *tableau vivant* acted before them;
swaddled in her spell, she can ignore them
who stroll untouched by how her life has withered
or what she might have been before she gathered
umbrellas, rags on the sidewalk, there to huddle,
daft old woman, an unwitting sibyl
in a city where compassion's stricken numb,
as though its prophecy of things to come.

[Darkening Water]

The City of Satisfactions

As I was travelling toward the city of satisfactions
On my employment, seeking the treasure of pleasure,
Laved in the superdome observation car by Muzak
Soothed by the cool conditioned and reconditioned air,
Sealed in from the smell of the heat and the spines
Of the sere mesquite and the seared windblast of the sand,
It was conjunction of a want of juicy fruit
And the train's slowdown and stopping at a depot
Not listed on the schedule, unnamed by platform sign,
That made me step down on the siding
With some change in hand. The newsstand, on inspection,
Proved a shed of greyed boards shading
A litter of stale rags.
Turning back, I blanched at the Silent Streak: a wink
Of the sun's reflection caught its rear-view window
Far down the desert track. I grabbed the crossbar
And the handcar clattered. Up and down
It pumped so fast I hardly could grab hold it,
His regal head held proud despite the bending
Knees, back-knees, back-knees, back-knees propelling.
His eyes bulged beadier than a desert toad's eyes.
His huge hands shrank upon the handlebar,
His mighty shoulders shrivelled and his skin grew
Wrinkled while I watched the while we reeled
Over the mesquite till the train grew larger
And pumping knees, back-knees, we stood still and
Down on us the train bore,
The furious tipping of the levers unabated
Wrenched my sweating eyes and aching armpits,
He leapt on long webbed feet into the drainage
Dryditch and the car swung longside on a siding
Slowing down beside the Pullman diner
Where the napkined waiter held a tray of glasses.
The gamehen steamed crisp-crust behind the glass.
I let go of the tricycle and pulled my askew necktie,
Pushed through the diner door, a disused streetcar,
A Danish half devoured by flies beneath specked glass,
Dirty cups on the counter,
A menu, torn, too coffeestained for choices, told

In a map of rings my cryptic eyes unspelled
Of something worth the digging for right near by
Here just out beyond the two-door shed.
The tracks were gone now but I found a shovel,
Made one, that is, from a rusting oildrum cover,
A scrap of baling wire, a broken crutch,
And down I heaved on the giving earth and rockshards
And a frog drygasped once from a distant gulley
And up I spewed the debris in a range
Of peaks I sank beneath and sweated under till
One lunge sounded the clunk of iron on brass
And furious scratch and pawing of the dryrock
Uncovered the graven chest and the pile of earth downslid
While under a lowering sky, sweatwet, I grasped and wrestled
The huge chest, lunged and jerked and fought it upward
Till it toppled sideways on the sand. I smashed it
Open, and it held a barred box. My nails broke
On the bars that wouldn't open. I smashed it
Open and it held a locked box. I ripped my knuckles
But couldn't wrest that lock off till I smashed it
Open and it held a small box worked
In delicate filigree of silver with
A cunning keyhole. But there was no key.
I pried it, ripped my fingers underneath it
But couldn't get it open till I smashed it
Open and it held a little casket
Sealed tight with twisted wires or vines of shining
Thread. I bit and tugged and twisted, cracked my teeth
But couldn't loose the knot. I smashed it
Open and the top came off, revealing
A tiny casket made of jade. It had
No top, no seam, no turnkey. Thimblesmall
It winked unmoving near the skinbreak
Where steakjuice pulsed and oozed. I thought aroma
Sifted, thinning till the dark horizon
Seemed, and then no longer seemed, a trifle
Sweetened. I knelt before
A piece of desert stone. When I have fitted
That stone into its casket, and replaced
The lid and set that casket in its box,
Fitted the broken top and set that box within
The box it came in and bent back the bars

And put it in the chest, the chest back in the hole,
The peaks around the pit-edge piled back in the pit,
Replaced the baling wire and crutch and oildrum cover
And pushed back through the diner, will the train
Sealed in from the smell of heat and mesquite
Envelop me in Muzak while it swooshes
Past bleak sidings such as I wait on
Nonstop toward the city of satisfactions roaring?
If I could only make this broken top
Fit snug back on this casket

[The City of Satisfactions]

Rats

To rid your barn of rats
You need a watertight
Hogshead two-thirds full
You scatter your cornmeal
On the water
Scattered as though all
The barrel held was meal
And lean a plank against the rim
And then lay down—

This is *important!*

—A wooden chip the size
To keep one rat afloat.
He'll rid your barn of rats
He'll leap into your meal
He'll sink he'll swim then he'll
See the chip
He'll slither aboard and squeal
And another rat beneath your eaves
Will stop
         and listen,

And climb down to that barrel
And walk that plank and smell
The meal and see meal
And one rat
He'll hear that rat squeal
I'll get mine he'll think and he'll
Leap in and sink and swim
He'll scramble on that chip

—Now watch him!—

He'll shove the first rat down
In the water till he'll drown
He'll rid your barn of rats
He'll shiver and he'll squeal
And a rat up on your rafter

Will hear,
       and stop,
           and start
Down the beam
Coming after
With one intent as in a dream—

He'll rid your barn of rats.

[The Center of Attention]

Egg

Now that Robin Redbreast
Has dropped an egg into her nest,
Round as the horizon, blue
As Heaven is, O lucky Egg,
There's only four or five things that you
Need know how to do:

1. Learn to hack your way out
2. To grow up (and master flying)
3. Finding out where the worms are
4. Copulation, etc., aerial
5. Nest-building skills

That's *it*. Everything else
Is optional, and who cares
For your opinions of your ancestors
Or views about the Great Redbreast
Who roosts at evening in the West?
The Future with its wrinkled brow
Will arrive regardless how
You try to flee, there is no place
But there it will reveal its face.
No more can you escape the dust
Than prove that Night, or Day, is just.
What's the use to weep or rage
Because all Heaven is a cage?
You have your how-to-do-it skills,
So don't peck at the world's ills.

[The Center of Attention]

Crack!

What was that?—The crack of doom or a sonic boom,
Bursting gas main or exploding furnace? A bomb
Set by guerillas mistaking the corner mailbox
For a pillar of the Military-Industrial Complex?

That tremor assaulting the soundtrack of silent dream
Only jostled the sharp night air. The dishes' rattling
Stopped before I had stifled my stifled scream
Or had the light on, or my mind working.

My wife switches the dark back on. We slip from shock
To sleep while deep below us, rigid rock
Blocks the insensate seethe at the core—We wake,
Only our curtains move, and the wind in the lindens.

[Hang-Gliding from Helicon]

Mother

Mother whose breasts were our green mountains
And whose assuring breath was scented summer air,

Whose body was the fields, the mounds, the valleys
It was our fortune to explore,

What happened? Your teeming valleys
Erupt in rash wounds, gashes. From sores

Vile fumes deaden the leaves. We are bequeathed
Your proud flesh, your powdered milk-of-ashes.

[Hang-Gliding from Helicon]

Ants

Theirs is a perfection of pure form.
Nobody but has his proper place and knows it.
Everything they do is functional.
Each foray in a zigzag line
Each prodigious lifting
Of thirty-two times their own weight
Each excavation into the earth's core
Each erection
Of a crumbly parapetted tower—

None of these feats is a private pleasure,
None of them done
For the sake of the skill alone—

They've got a going concern down there,
A full egg-hatchery
A wet-nursery of aphids
A trained troop of maintenance engineers
Sanitation experts
A corps of hunters
And butchers
An army

A queen
Each
Is nothing without the others, each being a part
Of something greater than all of them put together
A purpose which none of them knows
Since each is only
The one thing that he does. There is
A true consistency
Toward which their actions tend.
The ants have bred and inbred to perfection.
The strains of their genes that survive survive.
Every possible contingency
Has been foreseen and written into the plan.

Nothing they do will be wrong.

[Hang-Gliding from Helicon]

A Riddle

If all but one deny me, I am not.
The Greeks had gods for everything but me.
                                        Since then
How could I live on earth, in heaven? Yet see
If you can find me in the hearts of men.

[Darkening Water]

After God

The Jews have a Fancy, that when our Almighty Creator befpangled the Heavens with the *Stars of Night,* He left a Space near the Northern Pole, unfinifhed and unfurnifhed, that if any *After-God* fhould lay claim to Deity, a challenge to fill up that fpace might Eternally confute it.

—*Cotton Mather*

Who keeps His ceaselessly attentive eye
Upon the flight and fall
Of each Polaris through the wide feast-hall
Of the sky,
So like the life of man from dark
To dark in a little space,

Who in this bowling alley spins
Balls of light
At the back of the North Wind
Careening as their plastic skins
Mirror widdershins
Our sponsored images,

Who flings bright strands of platinum hair
And unpointed needles wandering
Through the frozen stratosphere
In a confusion
Of jagged rays
Until True North is lost,

Who deafens the Aurora Borealis
With climbing fire,
Who spurts with the desire
That blazes and subsides in ashen
Droppings of contagion
After the whirlwind,

Him we beseech
As adepts who would scan and preach
The Providences of His will.
Be done, send us a sign

That we may read
By the shrivelled light of our gelded sun

The sentence of our sufferings.
His blood flames now
Against the Northern sky.
He walks among us, visible.
The next dawn brings
A vacant hour that sacrifice can fill.

[The Center of Attention]

II

Aphrodite

How could she come to us inviolate
From that uncomplicated country
Of pure feeling? History

Alters all it touches,
And if her image now is such
That we cannot know

Which sacred objects her slim hands
Held, still, her glance
Resting a moment on our eyes,

Stays, then quickens with a clamorous beat
The bursting heart abandoned to desire . . .
If some goatherd with his rude

Mattock, or pillager's keen sword
Gash the cover of her mound
To seize her, as though mortal,

From memory's chamber underground,
The imperfections of her image
Are not her imperfections, the scarred

Seam, the limb sheared
By avid diggers or the gnaw
Of vandal centuries. Her face

Requites the tribute of our awe.
Her body's lithe, incomparable grace
Drives imagination wild

Should it please her to appear
As the one in whose embrace
The love that is engendered is beguiled.

[Broken Laws]

45

The Flutist's Breath Turns Reverie to Sound

The flutist's breath turns reverie to sound;
His hungering loneliness is music now.

Asnooze upon each other's breasts, the cottagers—
Half-harmonies they hear. Now each half-wakens,

The desolate skeletons of their selves lie bare,
The bonebox round each heart's a cage of longing.

Each beats alone and naked now. They hear
Woodnotes everywhere, and everywhere

The impenetrable hugeness of the dark.
Caught in the world's gizzard, they turn toward

Each other's loneliness, till face to face
A triumphant and companionable chord

—Coda to the flutist's monody—
They chant upon their fleshly instruments.

[An Armada of Thirty Whales]

First Sight

What you never knew was known,
Possession thought could not foretell,
Its recognition stops the breath—
Amazed, the beating heart arrests
And in the stab of that
Skipped beat
The soul leaps from its torpor, cries
"This is what you always knew,
This is what you've spent your days
Seeking in unknowing ways
As though the long procession of your days
Trudged obligatory paths
Across a dry waste of cold grey seasons,
So that you may acknowledge her"
—Not yet aware
What life it is of which she brings remembrance.

[Broken Laws]

Musebaby

Who put a mackintosh around
Venus of the Louvre? The pensive tilt
Of head, that hidden half a smile as though
Remembering a secret, and the downward
Sloping of the rounded shoulders—Yes, it was
On the Boulevard Raspail, when
From the Metro
You stepped, astonishing the day.

[Striking the Stones]

It Cannot Come Because Desired

It cannot come because desired,
It makes
Its own weather, its own time
Glowing
Like the phosphorescent wake
Of ships,
Mysterious tumult
Slitting the sensuous sea.

Love does not know
How we retrace
Together our most desperate seeking
Our most sacred place;

It's with these
Banal bodies
That we must
Make do,
Their strangely bulged and cherished
Curvatures, their folds, their flanks,
Their impermanent
Ageing surfaces
Concealing

Messages that we
Discover, each
The other's own
Rosetta Stone—

Love, I never hear
The brusque unpurposed clamor of the street
Or breathe the damp
Dolor that floods our city from the vast
Cool vats of space
But hold, an amulet against mischance,
Remembrance of your touch,
Your hands, your urgent hips,
The imperishable light, your sleeping face.

[Striking the Stones]

Yours

I am yours as the summer air at evening is
Possessed by the scent of linden blossoms,

As the snowcap gleams with light
Lent it by the brimming moon.

Without you I'd be an unleafed tree
Blasted in a bleakness with no Spring.

Your love is the weather of my being.
What is an island without the sea?

[The Center of Attention]

Night Fishing

You stir, or is it the first birds
Straining to open the darkness with their tongues?
You stir, you pass your arm behind my head
And we move closer, our hands find one another
As bodies slip together and thighs part—
In the dory I bend, bend to the oars
Exultantly, bend back and the boat glides
With its wake widening behind you, and the swirled pools
The oars leave as we slash through the bold water
Where the Head of the Cape juts toward the sea.
There you cast your line—its shining lure
Arches, then trolls from the rod held in your hands
Till there's a strike—the rod bends,
You whirl the reel as the caught fish darts and turns,
Rushes the keel and the line goes slack a moment,
Then, a slash of whiteness under the gunnels
—I've shipped oars and reach for the whipping line,
At last haul out of the froth a tinker mackerel
Flashing in the fading light all sleek
Stripes and slippery frenzy—I work the hook
Out of his gaping jaw and in the bucket
Plop him with the others. Grate of shingle
Under bow, we've hauled the boat up, gathered
Driftwood sticks. In the rocky cleft our fire
Glows and our green withes of new-cut alders
Spear the cleaned meat. The sizzling drips,
Drips on the embers. On a rock of snails
We feed each other flesh with the sweet tang
Of the sea, and the fire, and salt, as the tide breathes
Its long slow breaths along the shore.
We rinse our hands and faces in a pool,
The rumpled water stills, we see ourselves
Gaze back at us among the floating stars.

[Hang-Gliding from Helicon]

Alone

The convivial traffic of the evening
where I am stranger
strolls and rumbles over the bridge

across the river through the city's
heart, and now, in this
vast pub flowing with talking

among the quarrelers and reconciliations
and the lovers
lilting in one another's arms along the quays

I stand upon the footsoles of my shadow,
a shred of silence
tattered by the wind, by echoes

that fill an emptiness with emptiness
saying and re-saying
in your voice that I can all but clasp

all that we have said between us
while there was
between us but the distance of a breath

—more clearly still you come to me
and I lean toward
you, where on that rim of western sky

a jet plane darts across the veiled
moon setting
her cool fire into the wide dark sea.

A Marriage

"Remember that farmer down in Maine
Who said to us, 'I've been
An abandoned island
Since she's gone'?

—That's the hurt of proud flesh
We've known,
The heart's self-borne contagion
When you or I have parted us

With those rending, furious
Irretrievable accusations.
Each gulp of air keeps the wound fresh.
Left to the individual freedom

Of broken ends
We can't make meet, I roar
Off, a space-bound satellite
With no earth to encircle, adrift

In that unfinished void
Where nothing numbs the red scar
Of a burnt-out asteroid.
And yet I turn, seeking some tremor

Of your light,
Your heat,
Wherever in that emptiness
You are."

[Striking the Stones]

As I Was Going to Saint-Ives

As I was going to Saint-Ives
In stormy, windy, sunny weather
I met a man with seven wives
(The herons stand in the swift water).

One drinks her beer out of his can
In stormy, windy, and bright weather,
And who laughs more, she or her man?
(The herons stand still on the water.)

One knows the room his candle lit
In stormy, lightning, cloudburst weather,
That glows again at the thought of it
(Two herons still the swift water).

His jealous, wild-tongued, Wednesday's wife—
In dreepy, wintry, wind-lashed weather
—What's better than that ranting strife?
(Two herons still the roaring water.)

There's one whose mind's so like his mind
In streaming wind or balmy weather
All joy, all wisdom seem one kind.
(The herons stand in the swift water.)

And one whose secret mazes he
In moon-swept, in torrential weather
Ransacks, and cannot find the key
(Two herons stand in the white water).

He'll think of none save one's slim thighs
In heat and sleet and windy weather
Till death has plucked his dreaming eyes
(Two herons guard the streaming water).

And when to Saint-Ives then I came
In fairest, windiest, rainiest weather,
They called his shadow by my name.
(The herons stand in the quick water.)

And the one whose love moves all he's done,
In windy, warm, and wintry weather,
—What can he leave but speaks thereon?
(Two herons still the swift water.)

[The City of Satisfactions]

Reasons

Because when our clothes hung from the slanting alders
And summer the color of stream on wavering sand
Poured from the clouds, you waded under
Light-flecked glades reflected in the water
And repealed our exile from the Garden; because,
Seeing you of a sudden in the crowd
On Chestnut Street, the heedless, thoughtless plod
Of my heart was seized, and stilled, suspended
In another life, until
The beat of blood and breath resumed; because
While you're asleep the rhythm of your breathing
Sifts the air with a dark-flowered enticement;
Because when I grope through lightless labyrinths of despair
The unbroken thread of your love guides me back;
Because I cannot think of life without you
But as a season of ice and pain, of hunger
Without end; because in the candle-mold
I gave you thirty years ago, you've placed
Bouquets of pearly everlasting.

[Hang-Gliding from Helicon]

Who Was It Came

Who was it came
Over the mountains bearing
Gifts we did not ask?

—Not the sapience of the thrush
Or the ant's perdurance,
Something a body might use—

Who was it brought
Cerements and a wrinkled skin,
A sour digestion

Over the mountains, offering
Crotchets and a rheumy gaze
And wits gone wandering?

Just when we thought to repossess
The taut frenzies of Chicago jazz
And bridal ardor

Here he comes,
Inexorable gaffer in an old hat
Croaking our names.

[Striking the Stones]

Over the rim

Of this day hovers
The just design
This day tried
But failed to find,
All its busy creatures

Spurting with desires,
Spieling the recipes
Of their self-justifications
By which the mind
Of the entire world

This day betrayed
The perfection of our common
Lot, our clearest thought
Into these fragments, these
Wounds, self-serving anthems

And ridiculous longings—among them
You and I were for a moment
Together welded in a semblance
Of what this broken
Day left unattained.

[Broken Laws]

Another Border

Was it we who stumbled
Unawares across a border
Into a bleaker diocese,

Or did October's camouflage
Of crisp and primal colors
Infiltrate the parish of our pleasures?

No matter now
Who crossed whom, these colder
Wizened days that crowd us

And you and I
Thrusting impatient through their shorter
Gaps of lessened light

Move forward
Toward another border
—It must be there

Awaiting us,
That apostolic territory
To which we go.

[Striking the Stones]

Ignorant of Source

Ignorant of source,
Of consequence,
Love does not know
Its cause, its end,

Instinctually goes
About its business, opening
For a dozen minutes, maybe more,
The almost unendurable
Delight before
The closing once again
Of its blazing door.

Last night it opened as it had
Fifteen years ago.
That supersensual light
Made me father then,
And now we know
It's on our Father's errand
That we come and go.

Lovers into parents, we
Were transformed by love
Yet are the same.
Those who deeply think have said
That by the action of
A divine Love
The Unmoved Mover made the world.
Ever unchanged,
He must be changed thereby, begetting

New loves, new
Ways of loving, being loved.
Such reciprocities
Between what love creates and love
Were unforetold.
How could He know
His children would become the world?

[Striking the Stones]

In the Beginning

On the jetty, our fingers shading
incandescent sky and sea,

my daughter stands with me.
"Boat! Boat!" she cries, her voice

in the current of speech cascading
with recognition's joy.

"Boat!" she cries; in spindrift
bobbling sails diminish,

but Kate's a joyous spendthrift
of her language's resources.

Her ecstasy's contagion
touches the whirling gulls

and turns their gibbering calls
to "Boat! Boat!" Her passion

to name the nameless pulls her
from the syllabic sea

of incommunicate loneliness,
from the isles of infancy.

She points beyond the jetty
where the uncontested sun

wimples the wakeless water
and cries, "Boat!" though there is none.

But that makes no difference to Katy,
atingle with vision and word;

and why do I doubt that the harbor,
in the inner design of truth,

is speckled with tops'ls and spinnakers,
creased with the hulls of sloops?

Kate's word names the vision
that's hers; I try to share.

That verbal imagination
I've envied, and long wished for:

the world without description
is vast and wild as death;

the word the tongue has spoken
creates the world and truth.

[A Little Geste]

The Hill of Tara

for Kate

Curled in the corner, writing
In her Nine-Year Diary
Her own sentiments,
Our itinerary

(The moist wind seemed
Desolation's breath
On the chilled ewes and rams.
On that feast-hall's fallen hearth

Where queens lie still, the wind
Pearled grey lichened earth.
A bare oak swayed and keened.
The thornbush, on that heath,

Mourned in tear-streaked beards
Of last year's tattered wool.
None but the New Year's
Lambs leapt on that hill)—

"On the Hill of Tara
I felt like dancing,
And then the wind seemed to sing
So I danced to the song of the wind."

[The City of Satisfactions]

In That High House

In that high house half up a hill
A string linked your hand to my hand.
From the swollen sea that gnashed the shore
A road coiled round the hill's stone breast.
Our string pulls taut, frays, snaps apart.
The castle's ruined, a winter's tree.
You mustn't cry now, little son.
The rooftree's fallen and the moon
Through skeletal shadows lights the hall.
Beyond the broken door a road
Coils round the ridges of a hill
Where another house may stand
And your hand loop another hand
And when that filament frays and falls
In roofless walls remember us
When most together most alone.

[The City of Satisfactions]

Burning Bush

If a bush were to speak with a tongue of fire
To me, it would be a briar;
The barberry, bearing unreachable droplets of blood,
Or bristling in winter, rugosas with their red hoard

Of rosehips and a caucus of birds singing.
Come Spring, in a burst at the road's turn,
A snowblossom bank of the prickly hawthorn;
Or drooping in June on their spiny, forbidding stem

Blackberries ripe with the freight of the dark juice in them.
If I should listen to a bush in flame
Announce the Unpronounceable Name
And demand requital by a doom

On my seed, compelling more
Than I'd answer for, what no else would ask,
That voice of fire would blaze in a briar
I cannot grasp.

[The Center of Attention]

Folk Tale

It's enough to make one think they knew
Something, those old crones. At whose request
        Do they tweak baby's cheek with gnarled
Fingers? Who asked them, perched on every cradle,
To intone a blessing in their fireside cackle?
If we could only start out once without it—

Why is it that, when, as a new door opens
Toward an untried way stretching before us
        With limitless invitation, always
There's a staying hand weights on the shoulder
The sharp restraint of that remembered blessing,
Their admonition, You'll be most nearly happy

With a box you never open. Who then
Can think of anything down the road, the windings
        Unexplained, the paths, the houses
Deep in the woods, the trees startled with birds
And all made radiant with expectancy
—Who then can think of anything save that box

Because forbidden? Now at such a time
The guests have all subsided, their bottles spent,
        The drowsy sun itself falls silent.
Then night concludes the gathering for all
Communicants save lover and beloved
Who depart for haven to fulfill

Those rites for which these steps and incantations
The others witnessed were preludial.
        At such a time a barred door
Tantalizingly can open—Now
May they recall the wisdom of the tribe
Before it is too late, before it is

Too late. Something it was about an open
Box. Or was it not to open? No matter.
A meteor throbs, he thrusts its blaze
Into the darkness of the opening crack—
Her limbs melt, drops of tallow fall.
This is a tale that will be told again.

[Hang-Gliding from Helicon]

Ode to Joy

Your hand trailed over the hammock's side
And like a netted mermaid, you hung in air
Lending the net the langorous shape of your
Lithe body, and the curved air
Swerved around you bearing scents
Of old shrub roses and of new-mown grass.
I sat on the steps beneath the sun that poured
On sun-filled lawn and sun-splashed holly bushes,
Sun-crested trees, magnolias afloat where sun
Like a summer shower thrust itself upon
A glimmering sea. Each new breath I drew
Was joy—I knew no name for this delight
That flowed through arteries to crest, recede,
And crest again, as endless as the tide.
The grass below was a metaphor of gladness,
The beetle underneath its blades, a trope;
The earth still damp with dew bespoke its kinship
With the linked constellations of the night.
The ivy on the wall had shone forever.
Each object of our sight, each breath
Crowded with speech this love outlasting death
That flowed through me as though it would not cease
Ever to flow, and knowing this I knew
Nothing else there was that we need know.

That was before they pulled R. from the lake
At noon near Wilmington; before P.
Came down from the mountain, eyes glazed and mind
Blasted on LSD; that was before
G. had his stroke, then, rehabilitated,
Waited while the next stroke's fuse
Smouldered in his brain; before C.
Broke up with N., before their divorce;
Before F. grew old and grey and full of pain
And stumbled with a cane; before surgery for cancer
Left B. a little less each day; before
C.'s return to N. from S. and the ride
In the taxi when his heartbeat stopped and he died;
Before the wearing away and wearying of the body

As its possibilities wither and decline,
And among those present and accounted for
The obituaries in the New York Times
Feature those we knew as never before
While light seeps from a swollen sky,
Staining the foliage, the branches, the earth
Where by dint of looking I make out
A leaf, another leaf, so many leaves
Each with its own pattern of veins and greens
Hanging part of the way it hangs between
Its burst from bud and the oncome of a dry crackle
With which leaves stiffen, rub, and swirl
On the Autumn wind; by this dumb light
Shapes cast shadows and shadows grow
Until it is the twisted shades we know,
Shades that have no connection
To each other, or to the dark top hemlock bough
Where a last lone mockingbird, late straggler, pining
For the lost noon of summer, trills
His plangent repertoire, and fills
The evening air with intricate nets of sound.
Then magnolias, hemlock, hollies, eaves
Are drenched with falls of sweeter sound
Than they ever held before, as evening
Fades to dark save in the eastern sky
Where a flared moon lightens to a glow that brims,
Tinting the roofs, the tree-tops, and the ground
As though the gathered threadings of a bird's tongue
Could weave a tensile web that, hanging,
Holds the moon, and draws it up the sky.

    The very blackness of the air is laced
With light, invisible as the notes and catches
Of a moonstruck bird on a hemlock bough
Cascading from the deepest source of sorrow
To pierce the dark with momentary grace.

[Hang-Gliding from Helicon]

III

Incubus

What did the caterpillars do
last time the Phoenix died?
　　　They beat their breasts with a hundred fists
till one of them espied
the egg the ashes incubate.
Then, sure that wings would flame again,
they broke their bread on a mulberry leaf
and out of himself each wove the sheath
from which he'll burst on flaming wings
　　　after the peace of a season's sleep,
　　　after the peace of a season's sleep.

What did the little children do
when Christ was last time crucified?
　　　Each hid beneath a mulberry wreath
and on one another spied.
For they were playing Prisoner's Base
and as the teams hid face to face
the only thing that mattered much
was which was caught and which would catch
　　　before the evening grew more dark,
　　　before the earth and air grew dark.

[An armada of thirty whales]

An armada of thirty whales

(galleons in sea-pomp) sails
over the emerald ocean.

The ceremonial motion
of their ponderous race is

given dandiacal graces
in the ballet of their geysers.

Eyes deep-set in whalebone vizors
have found a Floridian beach;

they leave their green world to fish.
Like the Pliocene midge, they declare

their element henceforth air.
What land they walk upon

becomes their Holy Land;
when these pilgrims have all found tongue

how their canticles shall be sung!
They nudge the beach with their noses.

eager for hedgerows and roses;
they raise their great snouts from the sea

and exulting gigantically
each trumpets a sousaphone wheeze

and stretches his finfitted knees.
But they who won't swim and can't stand

lie mired in mud and in sand,
And the sea and the wind and the worms

will contest the last will of the Sperms.

[An Armada of Thirty Whales]

Cape Breton

There, there is a clearer air
that clothes the clouds
than any you have seen elsewhere;

the dust that hovers on the roads
across the roaring valleys moves
like genial daytime ghosts

over bearded reinsmen roving.
The firs are gnarled there, their tight whorls
beneath rich needles in the steep wind showing

despite the summer's benign warmth
that it takes courage in the storming winter
to grip this soil, and faith, and strength.

Valleys one's delight here are renewing,
and over every hill a valley dips
where goldenrod and freshets and the strong

rude grace of rock the ice has split
invite the eye and lure the roving eye
of broadwinged hawk down down to streak

birdward or rabbitward tempestuously.
Here, by beaches made of brambles and
shards of shale where somersaulty

streams spread clear cold waters under
hilltops hunched like shoulders spined with pines,
the village houses—wood worn silver—stand.

There is a style of living here that says
in the long barn backroof sloping to the ground,
in the frontal gable of the staunch farmhouses

that toward the road unblinking, forthright, gazes,
This life is hard but it's worth living.
Roads twist through forests where the logsled blazes

tributary roads, on forests giving.
Ride on, or walk; you are astonished
in a brutal wilderness believing

yourself to be to find schoolhouses
self-sufficient in the clearings
at the road's turn, each one bearing

a name: "MacLeod's School," or "The Widow
MacKenzie's School." Here education's
prized, here reading is a possession.

    This land makes strong men stronger. His
behemoth Barnum found here: Angus MacAskill,
whose wrists were thick as fir trees, yet H E W A S

A L O V E L Y G I A N T. What folk in the world have a hero so gentle?
Seeing themselves as a part of nature,
knowing their powers and the limits of their powers,

filling their backsloped barnrooves through the long hot summer
full of grain and lumber and rich hay for fodder,
they lay up against the cold grip, relentless,

of months like epochs when the world's frozen
and one might as well sit at the loom making an endless
tartan of thistles and rainbows and good wool woven,

while ice splits and the hawks scream and streams jangle
down down the glass valleys, till the winds wildly roving
blow winter away,
               and the clear air grows warmer.

[An Armada of Thirty Whales]

At Provincetown

Over the wharves at Provincetown
we watched the hooded gulls manoeuvre.

As one last gull, in late arrival,
flung his wings before our face

crying *"Wait!"* . . . *"Wait!,"* in a race
to ride their aerial carousel,

we saw his dark-dipt head, eye-bead,
each individual grace recede

as all swooped up, then spun, and fell
unmoving in motion. Here was pure flight,
free from all bird-appetite.

Then the highest soarer saw
the *Mary Magdalena* yaw
laden low with mackerel.

★   ★   ★

Over the wharves at Provincetown
the gulls within our arteries soaring

almost complete the great mobile
that all but froze gullsblood to steel.

Other wings across the harbor
flash like swords and dive for garbage.

[*An Armada of Thirty Whales*]

Icarus, Icarus

—(I've watched the preening
seagull's sudden leap from the pier's pile,

seen his elbows clap a cloud, careening
artlessly around the rocking steel

bell buoy. Cling, dong: monotonously
swivelled between the same unchanging waves

articulating rootedness. The sea
holds hungry stone. Tempestuously

the porpoise leaps, leaps, spreads his frantic fin
but snoutward underwater rippling falls—

On the rockledge, I feel my own back arching.
          An old beachcomber strolls in ragged sneakers

and faded denim pants halfpatched. His folly
is the sluggish village's diversion: acres

on the hill he lets run all to yarrow
while he caresses cast-off seagulls' feathers.

I think I know why his shrewd slant squint follows
invisible fulcrums where the tern teeters,

          and why the little boy in his Mighty Mouse suit
spread his arms and leapt from that high rock

—in the pure power of intensest wish he put
all faith—dying, he affirmed it, saying

"I flied, for a minute, just before I fell")
          —what ecstasy of pride it was that shook

you loose from all that beeswax & those quills,
O how you soared, that instant before Breughel

          showed human eyes unseeing at your fall.

[An Armada of Thirty Whales]

That the Pear Delights Me Now

That the pear's boughs
delight me now is
inconsequential.

But after fragrance come
bull bumblebees.
On ozone wings they hum,

on hairyhorny knees
rudely they enter,
nuzzle, gnash, & guzzle

nectar of the pear.
Roystering honeymakers,
wholly unaware

of the dust their bristles brought,
of the lovestrong draught
they pour down those pear-pistils.

It's June now, and the petals
have dropped, dried, crumbled,
in dust they've blown away.

Bees snarl in thick thistles;
pearboughs, hung in the hot day,
sprout green nubs now. Birdcalls

drench the leaves like fragrance;
fruit grows opulent in
summer lightning, heat, rains.

Sensuous the pears hang
richly, sweet and bursting.
Pears plop down. Birds follow, thirsting.

Nights nip the earthskin tighter,
sap stops of a morning,
sunred leaves more harshly flutter;

old pears the starling pecked at
wrinkle in the waning shade.
Fruit sourly lies, rejected

till it's out of the earth invaded:
maggots rapaciously & noiseless
fatten on fermented juices

and the gristle wriggles through
their sniggling tails & slime
spreads beneath the peartree.

   Some squush remains, though,
some meat around the seed.
When Indian Summer strains

the last warmth through the orchard
pearpits feast and feed
and stir, & burst, & breed:

Earthward plunge the tendrils.
   That the pear delighted me
is wholly incidental,

for the flower was for the fruit,
the fruit is for the seed.

[An Armada of Thirty Whales]

The Larks

An exaltation of larks arising
With elocutionary tongue
Embellish sound on morning air
Already fringed with scent of dung;
The curate in his curacy
Hearkens to that natural song,
And maids like wood-doves in their purity
Rise to matins' golden dong.
Their prayers are sweet high exultations
Whereon untrammelled spirits wend,
Forgetting flesh and breakfast. Under
The rectory eaves, the larks descend.

[An Armada of Thirty Whales]

The Clams

In the Bay of Fundy the clams
lie stranded, half-dry, by the tides

forty feet higher than sea
in killdeer's kingdom.

Underground, they erect valved snouts.
Wet freckles sprout over the beach:

Each trickles a droplet, and each
attests to the desperate hope

that attends each ritual drop.
Lie ten-hours-buried in sand

and the swirl of salt and the wet
seems an Age before suffering began.

All shrinks in the rage of the sun
save the courage of clams, and their faith:

Sacrificing the water they breathe
seems to urge the tall moon from her orbit;

she tugs ocean, cubit by cubit
over killdeer's kingdom

and ends parched freedom.
Moon, with sky-arching shell

and bright snout nine thousand miles long
and anemones in her kelp hair

that gleam in the heaven around her,
responds with the wave of their prayers

or sucks the sea unawares.

[An Armada of Thirty Whales]

Old Bug Up There

On Faneuil Hall there squats a copper
more-than-man-sized green grasshopper.

Impaled above the Farmers' Market,
snow-slow smoke and sleet have darkened

him. His mandibles munch the seedless wind.
No hunger's his, no brass caresses;

he leaps the rooftops toward no granary.
Lashed by acerb winds he spins

to point the way. But men are heedless.
        Old Bug, you remind me of someone,

like you above a city raised
to seem far larger than alive.

You're not the only one that's placed
on such an eminence. And if

fewer follow your globe-eyed gaze now
than when this harbor was spined with masts,

I'll tell you bluntly, you're not first
nor last to point out true unfollowed ways.

[An Armada of Thirty Whales]

The voice of the woodthrush,
played at half speed,

reveals to the halting ear
the fullstopt organ that pours through floodgate reed
such somersaults of sound like waters falling
in dark crystal chambers
on iron timbrels

withholds from what we hear
those haunting basses, loud but too deepkeyed.
This slow bisected bird's yet wilder calling
resounds on inward anvil:
pain is mortal, mortal.

[An Armada of Thirty Whales]

Auricle's Oracle

Intensity, when greatest, may
Prove ludicrously small.
Who concentrates compellingly
More than the snoutish snail,
Hauling gunless turret up
Perpendicular glass,
  By muscle of mind and bodily ooze advancing,
  Atop at last the aquarium glass balancing?

Yet passion at its most intense
Consumes the minuscule.
The focus of the spirit's lens
On whatever the self may will
Like sunlight squeezed through a reading-glass
Turns trash to flame. The ooze congeals
  In a golden signature of snail-identity,
  Etched in glass by the snail's and the sun's intensity.

[An Armada of Thirty Whales]

Shell

I would have left the me that was then
Clinging to a crack in the bark of the tree,

Stiffened in wind, the light translucent,
A brittle shell that had the shape of me;

And down the back a split through which had burst
A new creature, from mean appearance free,

Swaying now where the topmost boughs of the tree sway
At the center of the sound that's at the center of the day.

[The Center of Attention]

Ephemeridae

Dark specks whirr like lint alive in the sunlight.
The sky above the birches is disturbed.

Swarms swarm between pure heaven and treetops:
it's the mayflies' four-hour frenzy before their fall.

Waterward, they lay eggs in their dying
spasms, having then endured it all.

For five long shimmering afternoons that summer
we walked beneath the birchgroves on the shore

and watched the empty light on leaftips pour
and out of nowhere whirled the nebulae,

gadding gilded, all green energy, toward death.
After, the birches stirred, and we beneath

saw south-flying mallards bleak the air.
Green turns husk now. The world's shrunk to the bone.

Our thin flesh alone
through this long, cold, fruitless season

scampers frantic in wild whirligig motion
while larvae of the mayfly wait

and mallards migrate and the sap runs slow;
ours alone from time strains to purchase

pleasures mayflies find among the birches.

[An Armada of Thirty Whales]

The Everlasting

We went out on a meadow in a mote of the sun
waist-high in the yarrow
gathering pearly everlasting.

On the hilltop we gathered the luminous stems,
luminous flowers
cloudwhite as though holding the sun's light within.

We brought a full basket down the cow's-foot-plashed trail
where eared with a targe
a green frog disappeared in a hoof-deep pool.

That summer sped by as the corntassels climbed;
the patient dray, shod
where the smith's sparks gonged in the deep shed's shade;

the splash and shudder as the iced stream swirled
diving under the dam
bright pebbles and foam; the night-crazed loon

forcing his agony on the crisp dark . . .
The white everlasting
dried in the vase. By Christmas it stood

lightless and stark, prickly in pallor,
the husk of brightness.
The splendid energy of summer

glows in the everlasting still
in pearls of light
on yarrowy fields that scrape the sun.

[A Little Geste]

Exploration

I am who the trail took,
nose of whom I followed,
woodwit I confided in
through thorned-and-briared hallows;
favoring my right side for
clouds the sun had hemmed in.
Behind the North I sought daystar,
bore down highroads hidden
to undiscerning gaze.
My right, my right I turned to
on trails strangely unblazoned
where fistfive forkings burgeoned,
I took my right. Was destined,
among deerdroppings on the ridge
or chipmunk stones astrain
or hoofmucks in the swampcabbage
to err? Landmarking birch
selfmultiplied in malice till
woods reared a whitebarred cage
around my spinning eye. The spool
of memory had run out my yarn
and lost the last hank. Found
I the maze I wander in
where my right, trusted hand,
leads round and round a certain copse,
a sudden mound of stone,
an anthill humming in the rocks
an expectant tune?
Lacklearning now my knowledge is
of how to coax recalcitrant
ignition from cold engines,
or mate a fugue in either hand
on spinet or converse
in any tongue but stonecrop signs.
Clouds hump like battling bulls. The firs
lash me with angry tines,

shred my clothes. A windwhipped will
uncompassed, lacking fur or fang,
strange to these parts, yet whom the anthill
anticipating, sang.

[A Little Geste]

Safari

You need an empty burlap
bag; rubber boots;
a forked longhandled stick.
You need nerves like roots

of the willow half underwater
that stiffen the trunk they grip
though that trunk holds boughs aquiver
at the quietest breath.

You kneel on the willow's knees
probing the fern-rimmed ditch
till an arrow furrows the water,
till quiet is cleft by hiss

and quick and true the sinew
tightens in your arm, in your throat
and true and quick the long stick
lunges: a thunderbolt

pinions the diamond head
where the forking tongue is set
immobilizing nothing
else of that undulant jet—

I see those brave safaris
and my triumphal returns,
the writhing bag that dangles
from the forked stick's horns,

that dangles over the rosebuds
staked to the trellis I passed,
home through the tended garden
my prize held fast

—"To do *what* with those creatures?
You'll drown them in the drain at once!"—and dream
of a boy, rigid, goggling
down the manhole's gloom

at serpents hugely striding
in the diamonded darkness agleam
and thrashing the still black waters
till they foam and rise like cream.

[A Little Geste]

Climbing Katahdin

Hoisting yourself
From fingerniche to toehold,
Approaching the Knife-Edge,

A deep shagged ravine gapes on the one side,
The eye of a blueberry-silver pool steep
Down the dizzydrop other.

Your breath short,
Each rib rasping,
Grasping the thinned air above the timberline,

Clinging
To the desolate rocks
Below the snowline,

You can believe
As others have believed—
This stony ridgepole bracing

Heaven the longhouse of the mountain,
Ktaadn.
You breathe his breath.

Hoisting yourself
Atop the spined ridge you'll find
On a slight plateau

Stretching toward the peak's rise
Huckleberries growing
Beside a spring!—you laugh at the surprise

Of it and chew in the icy air
Bursting berries big as birds' eggs,
Your lips and tongue relish the purple—

Then arise from feasting
On silvery frosted fruit
In the desolation

To hoist yourself,
From fingergrip to toehold
Each breath grasping

As high up as the mountain allows you.

Eagles

When things are creatures and the creatures speak
We can lose, for a moment, the desolation
Of our being

Imperfect images of an indifferent god.
If we listen to our fellows then,
If we heed them,

The brotherhood that links the stars in one
Communion with the feathery dust of earth
And with the dead

Is ours. I have seen bald eagles flying,
Heard their cries. Defiant emblems of
An immature

Republic, when they spread their noble wings
They possess the earth that drifts beneath them.
I've learned how

Those savage hunters when they mate are wed
For life. In woods, a barbarous man shot one
In the wing.

He fluttered to an island in the river.
After nearly half a year, someone
Exploring, found

Him crippled in a circle of the bones
Of hen and hare his partner brought to him.
Close above,

She shrieked and plunged to defend her helpless mate.
Eagles, when they mate, mate in the air.
He'll never fly.

His festered wing's cut off, he's in the zoo.
They've set out meat to tranquillize his queen
And catch her too.

Who'll see them caged yet regal still, but thinks
Of eagles swooping, paired in the crystal air
On hurtling wings?

[The Center of Attention]

Before the Fall

The impersonal sun
Pours lambent fires
Through the fusty clouds,
Through withered leaves
Oblivious of the leaves
Or of the clouds' will,
Indifferent to our desires.

On amber shafts the leaves let
Light from the zodiac lean
Against the pruned hedgerows
Ablaze upon the lawn.
Midges, nits, and gnatwings
Sink and soar. Stray winds
Transfigure some with glinting.

Poised between the Van Allen Belt
And Catherman's Drug Store,
A book is in his hand
And he may cast adrift, may soar
On shafts of light, may bring
To his feast of shadows glints of sun
Before the Fall, or withering.

[Striking the Stones]

Blizzard

Nothing could stand in the way of its falling.
Day gave up the ghost to silent stormlight,
Like an autumn bear the sun slunk back in its lair.

Comfort and warmth, for those who remembered them,
Were compressed by the huge weight of the present,
Recalled like fossil leaves in stone.

Who could count how long the snow came down
While days were nights and nights were winter?
Time was trapped in the dark, in the icy wind.

Then the shape-shifting wind from the cave of the unseen king
Whose dominion is illusion
Rearranged bulk, expanse, surfaces, height

In the geometry of another country
Where we once had recognized our houses,
Trees, fences, gardens, roads.

When like ferrets we tunnelled out of our burrows
And blinkingly peered around us, dazed
And dazzled by the merciless shine,

On pathless ways through untracked nowhere
We saw relations of mounds and valleys,
Of no known objects in the one uncolor,

As purity poured into our eyeballs, with the pain
Of perfect whiteness where even the shadows
Are less white than white but of a whiteness still.

What could we do to reclaim the unfamiliar
And make it again into images of the familiar
With our clumsy mittened hands?

Yet, in less than a week, the tall drifts scattered
On aimless winds, and then, as the winds died
And rootmounds slowly sank and icicles fell,

Houses, trees, fences appeared again.
Now ruts are runnels, and under snowmelt
On the icy pavement footsteps linger

Of one who when the storm had just begun
Passed unseen and vanished. Now we reclaim
Our shovelled paths and unblocked roads, the shrinking

Snowpiles pocked with dirt. The earth despoils
With slush, soils the snow with sludge. This is our world—
We are earth's people, the earth's smudge is our sign.

[Darkening Water]

A Meeting

He had awaited me,
The jackal-headed.

He from Alexandria
In the days of the Dynasts,

I from Philadelphia
In a time of indecisions.

His nose sniffed, impassive,
Dust of the aeons.

A sneeze wrenched my brain
—I couldn't control it.

His hairy ears listen
Long. He is patient.

I sift tunes from the winds
That blast my quick head.

His agate eye gazes
Straight ahead, straight ahead.

Mine watch clocks and turn
In especial toward one face.

I thank Priestess of Rā
Who brought us together,

Stone-cutters of Pharoah
And The Trustees of

The British Museum.
When with dog-eared Anubis

I must sail toward the sun
The glistering Phoenix

Will ride on our prow;
Behind the hound-voices

Of harrying geese
Sink the cities of striving,

The fiefdoms of change
With which we have done,

Grown in grandeur more strange,
More heroic than life was

Or the dark stream at peace,
Or wings singed in the sun.

[The City of Satisfactions]

In Provence

A sky too hot for photographs,
A sky that bakes the toplids of the eyes,
A withered olivetree
That scratches at the crotches of the clouds
And on the rock
Among the sockets of the shadows
Lizards stop, and dart—

Here, amid the airs
Sweetened, pierced by wild
Thyme in heat, wild lavender,
It is the same
As under austere cranes that hoist
A frame of walls
Between us and the rigid sky

—The eye daring
Insupportable light
To find those slits in the familiar
Through which we peer,
Glimpsing then,
Or here, the only
Changelessness we'll know.

[Striking the Stones]

The Wastrel

This blear-eyed sun
Lurches down the horizon's
Street, deserted, cold.
He is himself the dull

Penny he beseeches.
Will no one help to fill
His empty cup?
Who'd think his gaze was golden

When he mounted up
The morning's tower of glass—
Then poised at the very top,
Profligate in air,

It was himself that made
What's paltry or despised
Resemble him. Each blade
Of grass he swathed in grace,

Dust blessed him to his face.
Dung shone in benison.
Who could forget that noon!
Yet who brings him its light

Now that his battered head
Totters down the road,
Or will repay the debt
Owed to spent delight?

[Striking the Stones]

Moving among the Creatures

Moving among the creatures
As the new light
Surges down this cliff, these trees, this meadow,
Brightening the shade among the alders
And shrivelling the dew on leaves,
They are contented in their bodies—I can tell it—
The squalling gulls delighted to be turning
Widdershins, their shadows swooping
Over rocks where startled deer
Clatter, flashing spindly shanks
And delicate hooves while underfoot
Even the uglies in their sticky skins
Exult, the woodfrogs clunking all the bells
In sunken steeples, till at my
Thick tread
They leap and scissor-kick away
While the withering leech,
Shrinking, enlarging, waving
Knobbed horns
Makes the stem shine
With silver spittle where he's gone.
I trip on vines, stumble in potholes
And long for something of myself that's in them,
In the gulls' windy coursing, in the frogs'
Brief cadenza, even in the slug's
Gift to leave
A gleaming track, spun
From his own
Slippery gut.

[Striking the Stones]

Inviolable

Horse, huge
On the hilltop
Leaning

Massy chest
To the open sky,
Unhaltered sun,

Meadows and
The hankering sea
Embracing—

O great
Creatures I would clasp
And nuzzle

Over the barbed
Wire fence
Though I trespass

My boundaries,
Breaking
Your laws.

[Striking the Stones]

Signatures

Wings outstretched, a horned owl
Nailed beneath a crown
Of antlers on the barn door

Shrivels in the wind,
And in the swale
Among black pellets,

Signatures of deer,
The wild roses of the field
—*Rosa Virginiana*—sway

As tall as trees. Each leafy bough
Beneath the deepest center of the sky
Is scented crimson as it's green with thorns.

There, on the sky's brim, floats
One lone jet too high
To break the day's long stillnesses.

Its white breath
Splits the sky.
The halves of heaven

Are bluer than each other.
All they cover leans to sign
Bequests of their significance,

Urgent as the center of the sun,
Yet silent
And invisible

As those fixed stars
We drift beneath
In the confusions of our light.

[Striking the Stones]

IV

Identities

One searches roads receding, endlessly receding
The other opens all the doors with the same key. Simple.

One's quick to wrath, the wronged, the righteous, the wroth kettledrum.
The other loafs by the river, idles and jiggles his line.

One conspires against statues on stilts, in his pocket
The plot that dooms the city. The other's a *good* son.

One proclaims he aims to put the first aardvark in space.
The other patiently toils to make saddles for horseless headmen.

One exults as he flexes the glees of his body, up-down, up-down.
The other's hawk-kite would sail, would soar—who has tied it to
        carrion and bones?

One's a Tom Fool about money—those are his pockets, those with
        the holes.
At his touch, gold reverts to the base substance.

The other's a genius, his holdings increase by binary fission—
Ownings beget their own earnings, dividend without end.

One clasps in a bundle and keens for the broken ten laws.
The other scratches in Ogham the covenant of a moral pagan.

One with alacrity answers to "121-45-3618?"—"Yes, *sir!*" The other
Bends his knee, doffs cap to man no man living or dead. One

Does all his doings as ordained by diskette or disk,
The other draws his dreams through the eye of the moon.

[Darkening Water]

O Personages

O Personages who move
Among me, why don't you
Guys come on call?
How can I serve the lost
King who, when the Secret
Service infiltrate the Ball Park
And the would-be assassin
Is paralyzed by the beams
Of their binoculars,
Paddles his paper-birch canoe
Where the sun's blood drowns the sea?

Musebaby, what good are you to me
In the dark spirit of the night?
Who needs you more than when the will,
Exhausted, finds dry clay
Where imagination's fountains were—dry clay;
O remorseless Goddess, you
Take your graces somewhere else.
Bleakness is bleak. And you,
Little Boy Blue in the velvet suit
My own Aunt Billie gave me when she came
Home from Vienna,

—You were fullsized, I was only three—
Where's that unquestioning insouciance
With which you bawled *Mine! Mine!*
Seizing all the candles on the birthday cake,
Eating them—Why do you fade
To brown, to tan, to nothing as
The rotogravure fades, leaving
Me alone with this bunch of motives
Scratching their armpits, gesticulating
From the crotches
Of leafless trees?

[Hang-Gliding from Helicon]

Himself

The one most like himself is not this mirror's
Dishonest representation
Of a familiarly strange person

Growing more crinkled around the eyes,
But one on whom he has not set his eyes,
One he knows is in this house with him.

In this very room there is
A youth he has outgrown, whose ease
With the world is greater than his own,

Whose gifts are greater than his gifts,
Whose joys are deeper joys
Than any he has known.

By the time that he began
To grow apart from that potential grace
He had never worn its face,

His callow years were all a waste
Of foolish choices and false satisfactions.
The blessing given him at last

Across the alien years
Is that he now may judge his actions
By what that one most like himself would do

Whose ease with the world shames his unease,
Whose delights exceed the joys he's known,
Whose gifts are greater than his own.

[Hang-Gliding from Helicon]

His Steps

You can just about keep pace with his
Skulking steps or leaps that tread your steps,
His back a sliver or dark hump by your side.

No matter how quick, how long his gait is
How supple his torso or how far
He leans away from you at evening

He will come back like a wild brother,
Linked in the syncopations of the light
As stolid theme and impetuous cadenza

Dance to the measure of the one song,
Or as a dream of flight that dares
Not leave its dreamer for long.

[Hang-Gliding from Helicon]

A Solitary

Oblique essence of the personal,
Your individuality's a hanged man on the neck
Of an albatross. O let the bird fly free,

That wide-winged soul has never
Shot a quill at you,
Murderer of your double!

Lacking companion, now
Exulting that you are unique,
You stake your camp on spiritual territory,

Not the human. Self-contemplation
Must be the range of your philosophy,
O bleak essence of the personal.

[Striking the Stones]

He Was the First Who Had Returned

He was the first who had returned
From that country
Of another tongue.

Speech, there,
Used purer forms of ecstasy than love
Here. Our actions fumble
With a gross vocabulary.

He makes the world
Around him glow
In simplicity of light.
His nouns are proverbs but their wisdom lies

Useless
In our boroughs of necessity,
Pure homage
Only known
When blood has crumpled, all its glories gone.

[Striking the Stones]

The Last Arrival

The last arrival in the furthest country,
All he saw he saw as mystery.
He to doorknob, counterpane and incised stone
That chanced to notice him appeared
Too familiar for comment.

And so they got used to one another,
The mysteries and the familiar.
In time all mysteries became familiars.
He in long familiarity
Disowned their secrets of their mystery.

Ceasing to notice him, they left as though
By prearrangement for the nearest country.
Someone will be the first to find that country,
In reciprocity for its reality
Will learn new names of all the mysteries

And write such full particulars in letters home
Unlike all correspondence known,
Since he with counterpane, doorknob and cut stone
Will parse that language of their own
To blurt out mysteries in ours, where all's familiar.

[Striking the Stones]

When My Wiser Brother

When my wiser brother
Who speaks so rarely
And only in my voice

(He is too busy matching souls
To the trees they will resemble, lovers
With one another,
The seahorse and the sun,
Sweet labor,
There's little time for speech)—when he

Finds words
Acceptable I will declare him,
For I am ready:
My phonemes, signs, parentheses
Await his spell.

All will be well
Disposed to consecrate the map
Of new peninsulas he will bequeath me.
But just when I've stepped out to choose the wine
For the banquet of our fond reunion
He will be gone,
Off to that republic
Of pure possibility
Where he plots a *coup d'état* against my exile.
Sometime, he may reveal it,

Though I am left meanwhile
Unbrothered,
My words all fled from split cicada skins
Into a busy fraction of the day.

[*Striking the Stones*]

116

The Way He Went

He didn't go away
To the roll of drums
Or to annunciatory thunder
Of mantic voices,

He didn't leave by the long light
Of line-storms slashing doomed horizons
Or the guiding blink and dousing
Of little harbor lights,

He went by darkness and by daylight going
A silent way
Vacating endless
Acreages of parking-lots and marshes

Still
Then evening all atwitch with raucous birds
Ignorant of the emptiness that fell
Lighter than dew.

He went
And the stars shone hard and rocks
Arose in their accustomed risings
From the sea while broken clouds

Scudded around and closed against
Ragged towers of a city
Gathering tumults of electric signboards
Glowing in the sky where many colors

Made one color
As before.

[Striking the Stones]

The Companion

Whether we come, in last imaginings,
To our earliest unremembered dream,
Or at the end it's still discovery,
Always the conquest of a final shore,

He will be waiting for me there,
As ever second-sighted and first there:
I groping my way in radiant day,
He cleaving midnight quick as flame;

He owns my features, favored gaunt as I,
Good luck's all his, yet he takes mine with me.
My tedious failures he disowns,
No place I triumph but it is his home.

[Striking the Stones]

118

A True Confession

Could I say,
Exalt the primacy of the id, the gonad,
the holiness of Me,
the electric ecstasy of those who go mad,

practice the absolute
freedom of the soul and beard to grow
and screw the resolute
endeavors of the mind to know

anything, because
in this senility of institutions
there are no laws
but beatitudes in the transfixions

of talented creators
who seek in orgiastic nurture
to liberate their meters
from the iamb's Chinese water-torture . . .

or, Could I say,
Ignore your senses, five unfaithful stewards;
the arrogant ego,
fallen on hard times, moves towards

imperfect submission
to perfect laws, and better had admit
its true condition
so grace may yet descend to it;

practice true numbers,
in strictness of the stanza find
the discipline that disencumbers
the featly gestures of a nimble mind—

O, I'd make poems and more poems every day!
One week I'd scan
all the Greek myths in a gospel way
symbolizing Modern Man,

next week, declaim "Epic Me!" out loud,
        all guts and gristle in a wallow
of words anarchic as a screaming crowd
        dismembering Apollo—

But it's no good. No, I can't violate
        my single double nature
and by reduction of myself, create
        either half-creature,

not even for a poem's sake
        sever nerve-ends from the brain
to think too purely and avoid the ache
        of ecstasy, or the throb of pain;

I'd be an undivided man who wields
        the contradictions
soul surmises and the cortex feels
        to speak in fictions

what truths of love or suffering I find
        in forms as fitting
as skill and will and luck combined
        may make, all half-unwitting.

[Darkening Water]

Vows

I meet him in the spaces
Between the half-familiar places
Where I have been,
It's when I'm struggling toward the door
Of the flooded cellar
Up to my crotch in a cold soup
Of my father's ruined account books
There, like an oyster cracker
Floats my mother's Spode tureen
(The one they sold at auction
When the market was down)—

Then just outside
Before I'm in the trooptrain on the siding
Spending the vivid years
Of adolescence and the war
With dented messkit in hand
Always at the end
Of a frozen chowline
Of unappeased hungers,
He appears—

Listen, kid,
Why do you bug me with your reproachful
Silent gaze—
What have I ever
Done to you but betray you?
To which he says
Nothing.

Listen, I'd forget if I could
Those plans you made
For stanching the blood
Of the soul that spread
Its cry for peace across the unjust sky,
I wouldn't give it a thought if I

Could only not
Remember your vows

To plunge into the heat
Of the heart and fuse
With the passionate Word
All thought,
All art—

Come, let's go together
Into the burning
House with the gaping door.
The windows are all alight
With the color of my deeds,
My omissions.
It's our life that's burning.
Is it ever too late to thrust
Ourselves into the ruins,
Into the tempering flame?

[The Center of Attention]

122

A Stone

Plodding down the road, past
A standing stone, scored, not
With distance to a destination
But the number that proclaims
How far I've come. It's always
When the earth is springy after
First thaw and the golden
Trumpets of forsythia
Are about to blow, I pass it
Going where I have to go,
Toward a stone casting its shadow
Farther down the road, scored
With parentheses, cupped hands
Enclosing half an emptiness
That awaits its filling-in.

[Hang-Gliding from Helicon]

V

Another Country

Coming to a cavern in a valley,
Who would not explore?
His pineknot lit, he thrust a way
Past droppings on the mossy floor,
Past walls that gleamed and streamed with waters
Into a chamber none had known before
Save who drew in colors deep as blood
The great creatures on that sacred dome
—Horned Huntsman, and the Woman, Moon—
It was then he found the doorway
To another country. Darkness
There is brighter than familiar noon.
The light that lights that land's like lightning.
Its sudden crackle rends the skies.
                              He tries
To tell a prospect of that country,
His words as much like lightning as the mutter
Of seared cloud
When the bolt's dazzle has come, and gone.

[Striking the Stones]

Evidence

On sandy floor, the evidence: thighbone, ribs,
skulls of antelope and deer, ringed by pawprints;
scuffed beside the circle of ashes, toeprints
and sticks with one end burnt, left where they'd been thrown
before some quake or ancient avalanche had
sealed this cavern—how many millennia
ago we cannot know till spectroscopic
test results come in on sample sticks and bones.
But we infer that this is where it happened:
The titan immemorial sabretooth
roaring his outrage, all defiance baffled
by wavering lights, by hot brands thrust or thrown
from his own cave's mouth where, erect and shaggy,
two creatures shout before the living, crackling
flames. A-dance on cavern wall, the quick shadow
of woman crouched at fireside, one hand holding
her swelling belly, the other clutching, closed
between her legs, the lid soon to be bursting
open. She yells encouragement to her mate
and his clever brother who, when lightning struck
the dead oak, with his flint hacked hot punk onto
a flat stone, and brought the smouldering ashes here.

[Darkening Water]

The Tale-Teller

Imagining a Father
Telescoped by time and distance nearer,
Larger, sitting at the bed's edge
—Beyond the sill the humpbacked branches
Conspire in cloaks; the gasping moon
Mints shadows on a desert floor—
But then the third wish of the seventh son,
A spindly cowherd with a knee of kibes
Who wears his good luck like a warm great-coat,
Flings open all the dormers and the night breathes
Companionable fragrance of new bread.
Branches flutter bannerets of birdsong.
The raggedy goosegirl claims her minion now
In golden gown and crown and silver shawl,
In all that empire theirs the one true fiefdom. All
That glowed between the grassblades and the moon
Grew luminous with love that spilled from them.
That's how the story ends. They loved each other
And their love like dew rejoiced the kingdom
And the teller of their tale
Was larger, nearer,
And his word was real.

[Striking the Stones]

Stop the Deathwish! Stop it! Stop!

—at least until the 21st century
because the present is too good to lose
a moment of—I would begrudge the time
for sleep, but dreams are better than they used
to be, since they enact the mystery
that action hides and history derides.
The past drains from the present like the juice
of succulent clams left in the noonday sun.
I spent the better part of my long youth
prenticed to arts for which there'll be small use
in whatever work the future needs have done:
I can file a needle to a point
so fine it plays three sides before it burrs,
or split a hundredweight of ice to fit
the cold chest with a week's worth in two blows;
is there many a man around who knows
by rote the dismantled stations of the El,
or that the Precinct House in Central Park
was once a cote from which the lambing ewes
and spindly lambs and crookhorned rams set out
to crop the green? In one-flag semaphore
I can transmit, or signal in Morse code
by heliograph such urgent messages
as scouts and sappers a boyhood ago
squinted through binoculars to read.
I still can cobble *rime royale* by hand
—and may, through now, about as few use rhyme
as wigwag or sun's mirrored beam to spell
their definitions of the ways that Time
endows the present it consumes, or tell
how only in this moment's flare we dwell
save when Memory, with her hands outspread,
brings back the past, like Lazarus, from the dead.

[Hang-Gliding from Helicon]

A Barn Burnt in Ohio

The night whitened in the bubbling light that poured
Out of the Milky Way, and in the pines
The massed voices of a million peepers sang
Whatever it is the stars to each other are singing

And then the silken glowing air was jabbed and torn
By the hoarse bellow of klaxon, the howling
Of firetruck sirens. Doors slammed like shots
And the whole village rushed to follow

The high red pumper with wood-spoked wheels, the scream
Of that pitched horn stabbing the clapboard houses
And the La France ladder truck gleaming, swerving
Through turns in the road between the curving fences.

A mile in the woods we heard the astounded voices
Of old boards snapped and twisted by great heat,
Felt the gibbering shadows of frightened trees
Leap and duck and turn at the wind's least twist and turning,

Saw the barn aglow, the cracks between the sidings
Liquid with orange and molten light. Then roaring sawblades
Of fire ripped through the roof on a suck of wind
And a great bellows beat storms of flinders skyward

As helmeted brigades with squirting hoses shrank
Back, back from the heat that pulsed out from the barn,
The barn a black outline still rigid in the fluxion
Of uppouring firestorm, flecks of hot ask flung on

Flapping tents of fire beneath a whirlwind sky—
It's forty years now since the old barn burned
In Ohio, and there among the villagers, some long dead,
I still stand still, silhouetted by that pyre,

Stand as the barn stood once while snow, a century
Of snow swirled past its eaves, where snow, where ash,
Executors of time's changeless will,
Sift down, till memory lose that ruined doorsill.

[Hang-Gliding from Helicon]

131

The Cape Racer

At the auction of the stuff
in the Staples' barn—ox shoes;
the kit for shoeing oxen;
a cider press; an anvil;
a hand-turned clothes washer; the box
of cobbler's lasts and hammers,
nails and rubber heels; a berry rake;
a double-boiler lunch pail
in which the lumberjack's boiled coffee
in the lower pan keeps from freezing
his sandwich in the pan above; a pitchfork;
another pitchfork; a lot of three
hay rakes; and a harness—resisting
all these as the bidders
responded to the auctioneer's
palaver, he an adept
insinuator of desire
in the hard-worked men who stood
under a light rain laughing
at his inevitable joke about
the thundercrock with a cracked
lid somebody bid two bucks for,
I nodded when he lifted and held before us
a Cape racer,

I who didn't need a thundercrock,
harness, hay rakes, lumberman's
lunch pail or cobber's lasts,
why did I want a Cape racer?
We're never here in winter
when the hill behind the farm is sheeted
with levelled snow and the tall grass
a mere stubble casting long shadows
on the unmarked tilt of crusted meadow,
but I could not resist the lovely shape
of the racer Horace Gray devised and made here
and named for this Cape in '79
of the century before the last, seeing
its length the height of a man

just one inch under six feet long,
its breadth a mere nine inches
—just wide enough to lie on—
the frame, on which the runners,
flat iron bands screwed onto bent ash rods,
support a boy four inches
from the whistling ground,
its twenty-two hand-whittled spars spaced
two inches and a half apart, no thicker
than your little finger, each one fitted
into holes drilled in the sleigh frame's upper bars,
and the racer held together without nails,
rivets, screws, or glue, the thing made taut
by tension of the twisted cords between
the right-hand frame and the left, cords
doubled and turned, turned with a sliver
of wood wedged
between pairs of the spars to hold it fast,
the sleigh so light one hand can hold it
in the air while bids are asked for,
so sleek it seems prepared for flight
over the clouds as well as the frozen hills

—the farmers and the lobstermen,
the lumbermen and berry-rakers
had no need for sleighs, so my initial
nod assenting to the auctioneer's
"Dollarbill, somebody bid me a dollarbill . . ."
has made me owner and proprietor
of a Cape racer I've never raced nor likely
ever shall speed down
the berry field and meadow with the grass tufts slithering
beneath my ears and the cut snow
whipping and stinging
numbed cheeks and reddened knuckles.
It's pleasure enough to see it lean
against the wall all summer,
as ready as ever it was to test
its lightness, strength, and taut design
on the crust of the bright snow or down
the white slope of the mind.

[Darkening Water]

The Hermit of Cape Rosier

The hermit of Cape Rosier has three houses:
One's atop the cragged bluff that leaps
splashing spruce out of the water, hackled pines
sawing a jagged hole in heaven. There
the hermit's house is: no door, windows like wounds,
a ribcage in a hat whose brim is eaves.
You have to know the path up there to find it;
even if you know the old back trail
you have to know the cut-off to the hermit's,
and when you get there, through the thorned blackberries
with the arched gulls shrill in the steep wind
you see   Keep Out   No Trespassing   assigned
on trees and staves. Perhaps you are not welcome.
"Hello! Hello!" The winds snatch "Lo!" and dash it
cragward, crumpled, down. A seahawk's nest
in winter, filled with lichen and picked fishbones
would be as hospitable as is this homestead.
Why would anyone not born to feathers
seek such isolation in the sun?
All that the senses touch up here is cleanly,
scoured by solitude in the harsh height.
Yet grant a hermit reasonable cause
to abjure our fendered comforts, still one might
search his self for the natural parts of man
in scenes more clement. Not the bleak of air
but ripeness of the earth, in summertime:
sometimes, beneath the blackberries, he searches there.

The second house the hermit lives in
some people wouldn't call a house, unless
sleeping in a cave's compatible
with the human lot. No one at Harborside
knows what got into Jarvis
crouching like a woodchuck in his tunnel
while a scourge of moles rips furrows his father turned.
He's got good lands back there he never touches
except a potato plot and a row of beans;
nobody knows why Jarvis won't be seen
at Meeting, store, or trade; nobody knows

just how he lives there, holed up like a marmot
while rains fall, and hay rises, and teams
move from field to field in hot July.
In woods, in the dead of summer, there's the smell
of green gone sour, of flesh the owl has killed;
delicate leafmould works its webbed decay,
a footstep stirs the leaves, and simmering death
bursts from earth behind a canopy
of green hands, giddy in the wind, that grasp the sun.
The cool of cave-mouth in the hill is dank,
the spindling spider hangs numb from his wheel,
the hemlock-guarded air is cold and still.

    The other house the hermit lives in
was once a boathouse, but he has no boat.
You pass clam baskets, broken, pyramided,
and mattocks worn down at the shiny tines,
split oars, stacked driftwood, a pile or two of shells.
Peering through the fogstained saltpocked window
imagine Jarvis fingering his trove:
great conches curling empty till his ear brings
titanic surfs to tunnels the silent snail
polished in solitude; bright rocks whose stain
of emerald or quartz shaft of shine the starfish
hugged beneath the tide.

    Death seems nearer Jarvis than it may be,
though in the village they say he's hale and sound.
Life seems precarious on his hillside,
battering windy breakers, by rot deepgnawed,
uncivil, ashake with joy and awe and wonder
at cragged Borealis
and the empty shell left on the shore.

[A Little Geste]

At Don's Garage

He ought to be hung.

But don't bother to call
the warden or sheriff,
they're of no use,
no use at all

since nobody actually saw
him, in rank midsummer, draw
a bead on that moose
—rotten shot, hit her in the shoulder—
nobody watched
as he didn't follow
to finish her off
where she thrashed,
blood pumping out of her side,
clots of red on her hide,
on the hardhack, the ground,
a trail wobbling back
through Camp Stream Swamp

till you don't need your eyes
to find her
belly bulged big as a balloon
nostrils noisy with flies
and a dead stench smothering
wild roses and the trumpet vine,

but some of us think we know
—we think of who we think shot that doe
and her fawn out of season
last month, and not for meat,
left them dead in the woods
just for the hell of it

—now would there be two like that in the same county?—

but if you haven't seen the deed, they say
it just don't signify. No way
you can testify against him.

You can only curse him.

Don called him a rottenlivered sonovabitch.

Virgil called him a yellowbellied bastard and made
reference to several serious defects
in his ancestry and breeding.

Bink called on God to pour
brushkiller in his beer.

We called on his chainsaw to jump
clear of the stump
and take his leg off,

we called on Camp Stream Swamp
to open its peat bog to his tread
and let him slide in the water and under the leafslime
up to his shoulders, his chin, his head,
let him holler awhile as he thrashes around
and gurgle then for a time
till the swampwater is still

except for the skeeters and whirligigs dancing
in the evening, when bullfrogs and peepers resume
the high tones and low sounds
of their old duet.

[Hang-Gliding from Helicon]

Old Reprobate

Old son, he said
When the fifth was nearly dead,
Your eyes look tired
As a dog's
Pee-holes in the snow.

One time the snow crews
Wouldn't clear his road
So he shaped him snowshoes
Like a bear's paws.
Where they'd plough, he strode—

It's been eleven years
And the snow crew still
Sees bear
In the woods, the brush,
Everywhere.

He'd say, I remember
Standing, as a kid
On that beach, holding
The horse's head
With the tide away out

And the rocks all rattling,
Sounded like a dancer
With castanets and heels
At the edge of the water
And Father pulling

The rockweed back,
Pitchforking lobsters
From every crack.
They'd twist like eels
Piled high on our waggon,

So many we'd strew
Them like manure
To make the corn grow.

On a still afternoon
I used to row

At halftide to the ledges,
Muffled oars,
Injun-like, slow,
Sneak up and grab me
A seal or two—

You ever tried
Seal steak, Dan?
Delicious, fried.
—But now
The seals are few,

Lobster's scarce,
There's been no bears
In a dozen years.
He's the game warden
And our fifth is gone.

[Hang-Gliding from Helicon]

Lines for Scott Nearing

(1883–1983)

And what if you were wrong about Albania?
You called child labor Capitalism's disease
While children toiled in the coalmines of Trustees
Of the University of Pennsylvania,
Who fired you from their Wharton School forthwith—
A *cause célèbre!* Our tenured free speech grew
Out of "the Nearing case." But not for you,
Old rebel loner, bound to Reason's myth—
The economy is just that is all planned.
Was this what in your old age drew the young
To your walled garden, as witness to a life
Of Thoreau's abnegations, though with a wife?
Your rows of Escarole, Romaine, Deer's Tongue
—How comely, how proportionate your land.

[Hang-Gliding from Helicon]

Scott Nearing's Ninety-Eighth Year

Shsh, Zzzzz; Shh, Zzzzz:
from behind the stone house the hissing
of the bucksaw's blade in rhythm
as though the day is drawing breath—

there, at a sawhorse between two rows of cordwood
stacked five feet high and longer than the house is,
he, at ninety-seven, is sawing, sawing
a twisted gnarl of maple

—of course I grab the other end and pull.
He pulls, I pull, he pulls, and the teeth
sizzle, sizzle, as the crack spits
white sawdust to the ground, until

we have to turn the knotted chunk, so heavy
it nearly topples from the sawhorse, to change
our angle of attack. Scott grasps a wedge,
slips it in the crevice, taps it

with a maul. No go. He knocks it out
and now we saw again. I'm in a sweat,
this day is hotter than I'd thought.
On either side of us stand wagonloads

of well-split cordwood. Why are we toiling, toiling
to cut into stove-sized logs a recalcitrant
knot—has this old man spent all his life
gnawing intractable problems, so can't now stop?

"When we've finally cut this thing in pieces
small enough to fit into your stove,
how much warmer will it make your house?" I asked,
as he pulled, and I pulled, and he pulled the saw.

"That's not the question," he said, sliding
the bucksaw free, then slipping in the wedge again.
"Each stroke" *(tap-tap)* "is a lengthening" *(tap-tap)*
"of life"—as the gnarl split and the wedge clanged

on the ground. Now Helen calls me to come in and see
how the last book she's written begets another book,
while Scott puts bucksaw, maul, and wedge away
in each appointed place. In the Franklin stove

a log smoulders. He lifts a yard-long tube,
breathes on the sullen embers—red,
yellow flames dance, spread feathers from the ash
arising from their last night's fire.

Bob

Hadn't been out of the house, except
once a week to the hospital, since
that day three months ago when they brought him
home from the mine, doubled over
in pain, no longer breathing acid fumes
or dust from the schists the copper ran in,
but sick, sick inside. So I didn't expect
while scraping and sanding my hourglass puller
tipped keel-up above the tide-line
to see come, slowly down the hill
to the beach road, his big green pickup
with the front hitch for a snowplow and movable
spotlights on the cab, and him
driving. He stopped, rolled the window down,
looked out and said, Be sure you caulk
those seams around the keel. Beside him
Katherine gave a wan smile. Then, toward us
came that little red Toyota
of Hobie's, who'd had hard words from him
two winters past about cutting wrongside
of the line between their woodlots. Since then
they hadn't spoken, but Hobie stopped,
leaned from his window and called out, Hey there!
Good to see ya! D'ya know the mackerel
are running? My boy hauled in a bucketful
at the town wharf last night. And next
Bing's empty dump truck roared and rattled
across the beach, then stopped, blocking
the road—Hiya (as though they'd spoken
only the day before)—We've finished
roofing that house on Varnumville
—talk whittled down to the dailiness
of living and the expectation of
tomorrow. I said, If you don't stop by,
Liz will be disappointed. So I got in
beside them. He winced, putting the truck
in gear. It rolled up to our drive.
At the table by the window we watched
the cove's arms embrace sun-deckled water

stirred by cat's-paw breezes as the gulls
swooped and terns dove. You can see
thirteen islands, he said, from here
(and, as his father had done for us
a quarter-century before, he called
their roll)—Pond Isle, and Beach,
Butter, Colt's Head, Horse's Head, North Haven,
Eagle Isle, Western, and Resolution . . . He said
the names as one who tolls his beads
before leaving on a long journey
so that never would he forget
this place, these islands,
wherever it is that he'll be gone.

[Darkening Water]

VI

I Am the Sun

I am the sun the sun says
All that's scorched beneath my eye
Is mine   We were just going the winds sigh
What will become of us the leaves cry

Nowhere to go mutters the maple
Grizzled in its skin of wrinkles
What will become of us the lovers
Do not think to wonder in the dappled

Sun thrust through the wind-tossed leaves
Where head on breast and thigh at rest on thigh
Find such delight they'd take the world for love's
Body that cannot change or die

[Broken Laws]

Aubade

Weaned from moon
By whitening sky

The still cove
Swells as the tide fills

There is no quenching water's
Thirst for light

Summer Solstice

Who's to tell the night heron
This night merits his observation
Or inform the carpenter bee
Of the day's singularity?

Only the membrane in the tissue
Of the algae or the eye
Steeped in ancestral memory
Retentive of stimuli

Has that calendrical
Instinct by which in France
On this day children strew the road with petals
Men burn a paper goat the women dance

[Broken Laws]

Singing

This season
Belongs to the creatures
Peepers claim the nights

Sparrow thrush and skreaking waxwing
Extrapolate toward morning
Their cadenzas of a gilded day

Instinctual calls whose importunity
Pleases as though the webbed
Desirous song and aubade of the swamp-sparrow

Were notes that we remembered singing
Once, and years after
Recollecting how to sing

[Broken Laws]

The Sounds

No use to make a tape
Recording of the liftoff
Or incorporate the sounds

The oil rig emits
In our suite—not
These the true ground

The ordained cadences
For rendering the thought
Which music is

Suggested by vestigial
Bird's whistle now or wailed
Snatch on boy's harmonica

[Broken Laws]

The Gift of Tongues

I the Scop of my own Saga
You the Epic Hero of your Epic
She the Lady of her Sonnet Sequence
—What will become of us

Now all the forms are broken,
Jibberjabber written, spoken,
Automation causing traffic jams?
Virtual employment bursts the till

In the Shop-'N'-Save.
America really moves the goods,
America's got the goods. Nothing's for free.
Who needs the gift of tongues?

[Darkening Water]

Speech

It's hard to tell which
of his cluckings and gnashings
are consonants for sure.
Not easy, though you try

to make out his vowels
from the slurps, to distinguish
among noises, words.
But the fellow wants to communicate,

he has things on his mind to say.
So wherever he goes he carries
an alphabet on a folding board.
You'd think it was chess or backgammon.

and if he'd sit still for a minute
and keep his head from lolling
it would seem he is wild about games.
He has stumbled onto the bus,

he's sprawled in an empty seat.
Now he points a twisted finger
to one, then another letter.
The woman beside him looks around her.

He thrusts the board before her.
His limbs have lives of their own.
Should she move to another seat?
Strange gurgles come out of his throat.

Everyone's looking at her.
Why does he want her to look
as his forefinger gropes toward the J?
Of what is it that she is afraid?

Now his finger crawls back to the box
containing the E, and stops,
She watches it lunge to the S
while the skin around his mouth

stretches in sideways smile.
His thumb seems screwed on backwards
but the forefinger jerks back and forth
as she sits perfectly still

to U and returns to S
and lurches away and returns
to S and the woman beside him
has all this while been bemused

to know what he was doing.
But that's not the problem now.
She can guess what he's trying to say
but not what she should reply,

or how to address a creature
in such a case—should she speak
with especially slow
and clear enunciation

so he could read her lips?
She knows she has only the time
he takes to fumble and find
the A, the V, then E

and S to make up her mind.
Later she will recall
she wasn't afraid at all.
It was like talking to someone

who is wearing a strange disguise. "Yes,
that's true"—her words once out,
his body for a time is still
as is one who is eased of his burden.

[Darkening Water]

The Peaceable Kingdom

The Phi Beta Kappa Poem,
Swarthmore College, 1964

I

Now that we sponsor the extirpation of folklore,
    The growing scarcity of trees,
Bulldozers gouging roadbeds through the valleys,
    Traffic clogged where streams once flowed,
More people nourished by more Inplant Feeding,
    The disuse of Deer Crossing signs,
Proliferation of home-heliports,
    Attrition of the harvest-home
And slagheaps overshadowing the city,
    The mountain's heart quarried away,
Ingurgitation of knowledge by computers
    Whose feedback gives for wisdom facts
Elicited by robots or commuters
    Grown unhandy with real things
From much manipulation of abstractions,
    The seasons seldom touching them,
Not even benign falls of snow disguising
    A land it will be harder to love;

Where Opulence, demotic *arriviste,*
    Counts his costly toys like beads
While Penury gnaws knuckled fists, her brawling
    Brood of brats picking through trash,
The sullen disinherited and darker
    Faces massing in the square
As though impatient with their ill provision
    Despite the auspex of Dow Jones
That proves the National Gross Product growing,
    The deserts paved with fresh concrete,
Rumbling shadows of the freightcars tilting
    From mine to mill to guarded zone
And skies athrob with gaud and roar of firework,
    Gigantic needles jabbing high
Swiftly trailing flame like thread, then piercing
    The beady button of the moon,
Ashes on Wyoming's fodder falling,
    Milk curdled, stunted seed;

155

II

are we ready to go forth? Where you have come from
the students will be ever young; there it is only
the faculties and trees grow older. Leaving this friendly
hillside, you will reach your destinations—be sure
in your luggage, among trophies, clothes, and lists
of those Important Books as yet unread, to bring
the Catalogue of the Ships and tales of revolution
—the Russian, the Industrial—and explications
of both the valence table and the vertebrates
who, since the Good Duke dreamed a green world where the court
corrupts no man, agree upon hypotheses
that define the Good and tell the False from True.

III

Imperfect learning, bless this place
With possibilities of grace.
Let Mind, that ranges Heaven as far
As Barnard's pendant, lightless star,
Regard, though darkness shroud the soul,
Its constant living aureole
That casts one comprehending light
Across our chaos and the night;

Transform the deserts abstract thought
And unslaked selfishness have wrought
Into orchards where the trees
Stand rich with fruit, epitomes
Of sensuous joys that leap from birth,
Nourished in the dark of earth,
Toward sapling vigor crowned with flowers,
In acts as self-fulfilled as ours

Who build a city out of stone.
And in whose image is this done?
Defend our visionary quest,
Humane intelligence, that we
Who've eaten fruit from nature's tree
And know perfection but in art,
May, schooled and chastened by our past,
Conceive our city in the heart.

[Striking the Stones]

156

On the Industrial Highway

Approaching the Walt
Whitman Bridge you pass
an affluent world—

a subculture of spouts,
nozzles, ducts, a host
of snakes and ladders

in nests and thickets
or by tribes, laying
dinosaur farts

against the sun.
I drive slowly through the
stink and gawk at

shapes that no
familiarity breeds,
a ghostless city

called "gas works," never
meant for death or living.
A pipe pulses

flame in secret
code on the gashed sky.
Here are things

whose archetypes
have not yet been dreamed.
There's no more perfect

duct than these
ducts, pipes, facts
burdened with nothing

anticipating
unhappened memories,
visionary things.

[Striking the Stones]

The Center of Attention

As grit swirls in the wind the word spreads.
On pavements approaching the bridge a crowd
Springs up like mushrooms.
They are hushed at first, intently

Looking. At the top of the pylon
The target of their gaze leans toward them.
The sky sobs
With the sirens of disaster crews

Careening toward the crowd with nets,
Ladders, resuscitation gear, their First
Aid attendants antiseptic in white duck.
The police, strapped into their holsters,

Exert themselves in crowd-control. They can't
Control the situation.
Atop the pylon there's a man who threatens
Violence. He shouts, *I'm gonna jump*—

And from the river of upturned faces
—Construction workers pausing in their construction work,
Shoppers diverted from their shopping,
The idlers relishing this diversion

In the vacuity of their day—arises
A chorus of cries—*Jump!*
Jump! and *No*—
Come down! Come down! Maybe, if he can hear them,

They seem to be saying *Jump down!* The truth is,
The crowd cannot make up its mind.
This is a tough decision. The man beside me
Reaches into his lunchbox and lets him have it.

Jump! before he bites his sandwich,
While next to him a young blonde clutches
Her handbag to her breasts and moans
Don't   Don't   Don't   so very softly

158

You'd think she was afraid of being heard.
The will of the people is divided.
Up there he hasn't made his mind up either.
He has climbed and climbed on spikes embedded in the pylon

To get where he has arrived at.
Is he sure now that this is where he was going?
He looks down one way into the river.
He looks down the other way into the people.

He seems to be looking for something
Or for somebody in particular.
Is there anyone here who is that person
Or can give him what it is that he needs?

From the back of a firetruck a ladder teeters.
Inching along, up up up up up, a policeman
Holds on with one hand, sliding it on ahead of him.
In the other, outstretched, a pack of cigarettes.

Soon the man will decide between
The creature comfort of one more smoke
And surcease from being a creature.
Meanwhile the crowd calls *Jump!* and calls *Come down!*

Now, his cassock billowing in the bulges of Death's black flag,
A priest creeps up the ladder too
What will the priest and the policeman together
Persuade the man to do?

He has turned his back to them.
He has turned away from everyone.
His solitariness is nearly complete.
He is alone with his decision.

No one on the ground or halfway into the sky can know
The hugeness of the emptiness that surrounds him.
All of his senses are orphans.
His ribs are cold andirons.

Does he regret his rejection of furtive pills,
Of closet noose or engine idling in closed garage?

A body will plummet through shrieking air,
The audience dumb with horror, the spattered street . . .

The world he has left is as small as toys at his feet.
Where he stands, though nearer the sun, the wind is chill.
He clutches his arms—a caress, or is he trying
Merely to warm himself with his arms?

The people below, their necks are beginning to ache.
They are getting impatient for this diversion
To come to some conclusion. The priest
Inches further narrowly up the ladder.

The center of everybody's attention
For some reason has lit up a butt. He sits down.
He looks down on the people gathered, and sprinkles
Some of his ashes upon them.

Before he is halfway down
The crowd is half-dispersed.
It was his aloneness that clutched them together.
They were spellbound by his despair

And now each rung brings him nearer,
Nearer to their condition
Which is not sufficiently interesting
To detain them from business or idleness either,

Or is too close to a despair
They do not dare
Exhibit before a crowd
Or admit to themselves they share.

Now the police are taking notes
On clipboards, filling the forms.
He looks round as though searching for what he came down for.
Traffic flows over the bridge.

[The Center of Attention]

The Great American Novel

I have spent most of my life
Gathering material.

Autumn. I am learning to balance
My brand new bicycle. Under
The pin oak, Father
At a collapsible table
Sits on a folding chair.

The tale is as long as the slow
Braiding of Mother's black hair.

No matter how often he harrows
His pencil down the columns
The total is always the same,
The same parentheses always
Enclosing (Loss).

[Hang-Gliding from Helicon]

Possession

You were sleeping? That's the time you're
Likeliest to hear my rat–tat–tat–tat–tat
Beat upon the pane between
Your self and your desire. The breeze

Baffling the leaves of your thought
Grows harsher, colder. This chill
Wind that clamps your veins
Is fanned from the black feathers

Of my outstretched wings. Of your wings.
Half-awake
You feel yourself reclaim the shape
You took before you took your shape.

[Hang-Gliding from Helicon]

A Dreamer

Awakened by the clarity of dream
As the train pitched forward in a rush careening
Down the mountain—Who wouldn't scream
When brakes fail and the conductor
Leaps from the hurtling car? It was good,
Good to clutch the reasonableness of terror,
There was reassurance in that real
Fall, real crags, a landscape of sensible
Disaster, not this nameless, numb
Dread, the humming sun a poisoned stinger.

[Broken Laws]

A Dread

It can be practically nothing, the nearly invisible
Whisper of a thought unsaid.
Pulsing, pulsing

At the bland center of a blameless day
It spreads its filaments through the world's
Firm tissues,

Relentless as an infection in the blood
Of one's own child, or a guilt
Time won't assuage.

[The Center of Attention]

A Woe

Larger than the sky
That squats upon the vast horizon
There is a woe

Pressing down
On this house of stone.
It thickens in the air of this room.

It is as though
One loved as much—no, more—
Than oneself were trying

To thrust away
With small hands
Stifle of the heavy air

While in the dark
I lie
Pinioned, all my strength

Useless to prize
The weight of heaven
From her eyes.

[The Center of Attention]

The Summerhouse

Climbed uphill to the seashore summerhouse,
Domed and shingled cottage occupied
By certain predecessors in whose pots
Our porridge bubbles merrily. The waves
Crash beyond the windows. Without ceremony
They pack their things and are about to go.
Well, we will soon forget them walking
Dourly without shadows two by two.
It's our vacation, sheets dried in the sun—
Out from the floorboard, underneath the bed
With slightest scrape of scale on wooden grain
The flattened head of a silent copperhead
—A kitchen cleaver leaps into my hand,
Shining through the high song of your fear
The whacking silver arc of light descends
And head rolls, chomping, and the lithe
And lovely diamonds down the back writhe.
He, he, tall, returns, removes
A curved and grooved tooth and squeezes it
Into my palm.—"Here, it's yours now."—"Thanks,
But might I not, as a memento, keep
The head?"—"Oh, no, there's poison in the fangs."
And now he's dropped the snake into his thermos
Of iced tea ("The place is yours") and driven
Down the sinuous twisting distant road.
And we've the sunny, salty, freshened air
And wind-dried linen sheets to spread.

[Striking the Stones]

Evening

As a corpse
Bleeds
In the presence of its murderers

The scars
Of this grey sky
Burst again,

The wounds
Gush. On our hands
The stain.

[The Center of Attention]

Brainwaves

When his head has been wired with a hundred electrodes
Pricked under the skin of his scalp and leading
Into the drum of intricate coils
Where brainwaves simulate motion

In a finger so sensitive that it can trace
The patterns of idiosyncracy
Which, without his knowing or willing,
Are the actions of his mind.

He is told to lie down on the cot and the current
Begins to flow from his brain through the hidden
Transistors. The needles on the dial veer,
The finger makes a design.

The attendant is reading the dials, no more
Input than from a distant star,
Its energy pulsing for millions of years
To reach the electroscope's cell.

He lies there thinking of nothing, his head
Hurting a little in so many places
He can't tell where. If the current reverses
Direction he'd be in shock,

But the pulsing of twitches and their subsidings
Flow toward squared paper. Is it good
For a man to be made aware that his soul
Is an electric contraption,

The source of his dreams a wavering voltage
From a battery cell—such a piece of work
That the stars in their circuits are driven through space
By an analogue of its plan?

[The Center of Attention]

168

Thought I Was Dying

Like a bucket
With a hole

I couldn't find
Just felt the seeping

Of my life
As it was leaving

My wife my children
Drifting away

My head empty
My hands my heart

Drained and void
The bed cold

I thought it's hard
To leave my life

With each breath
A little less

In the veins whistling
Till the sun shone black

As though I never
Could come back

[The Center of Attention]

A Resurrection

When I arose I knew I had been dead.
My fingers and my lungs still gray with clay,
Before my eyes a gleaming world unrolled.
Behind, the dark curled deeper in its cell.

What cold grip clutched my back? Moldy breath
At each gulp clearer, warmer . . . I am forgetting
The long impenetrableness of death
Beyond remembrance and past all forgetting.

Coffee! OJ! Let this day be a boon!
In clarifying light in freshening weather
Memory revives—the future is its gift

While shadows of tall clocks shrivel in the sun.
I'll plunge into the maelstrom of our swift
Redemptive life, for there may be no other.

[Darkening Water]

Emblems

When the mandibles of the clock have gnawed
The journal of another day,
So many drawn breaths nearer
A next incarnation,

I find in that no solace.
My enterprise dissembles nature's plan.
I would hold age in stiff abeyance
And command time's watchdog to obedience

To the intensities of joy. A windy
Cloudless day of dolphins around a dory,
Beachfire, the surge, the wildness of the sea,

And secret fissures of one woman's love
—Among the emblems I array to daunt
Too swift precessions of the moon and sun.

[Darkening Water]

VII

Fables

What does it matter that the tales are lies,
That a lad like none the villagers had known,
Meeting a poor old man at the crossroads, shares
Half his own crust, not, like both his brothers
Bidding the beggar with curse and kick begone,

The beggar who fills the boy's noggin with the need to bring
A drop of water from the Well at the World's End home
(Just so as to find what good may come of it),
With no man to point the road to the end of the world
But only Earth, and Sea, and Sky to send him

Forth to thwart the Crone, the Giant, the Sea-Troll
Who would prevent him, but since his heart is pure
He will be aided—a talking horse befriends him,
A dolphin, and a sparrow with second sight
Reveal the gifts to help his quest perdure,

The stone that will not miss whatever it's thrown at,
The cloak he walks invisible in, the feather
That the winds waft always toward the World's End
Where at last he'll dip his jug in that clear well
And sail for home with a teardrop of its water,

Holy water his good luck brims in, beaching
In a far demesne whose princess he will marry
And take in his craft by winds borne to this village
Where all the folk remember him, and he
Will lead his bride to bed, but first they tarry

And harken, by the embers, to the stories
Of a lad like none the villagers had known,
Who shares his crust with a beggarman so wise
He sends him forth to find his fate alone
—What does it matter that the tales are lies?

[Darkening Water]

175

On First Looking into Lattimore's Homer

With smaller Latin and less Greek
Than Keats, I had to roam
With those who rowed on perfumed seas.
My trireme was launched in the Eighteen Nineties,
The wrath of Achilles but a tinted scene
On tapestries
Embroidered, unreal,
In a language none could feel or speak.

Now the seas snarl where an arrogant keel
Supple through swell and spume
Dares tread the god-infested Mediterranean.
See doom-bound Hektor, eager to assuage
Blood-maddened rage—
How we are torn,
Whether to exult or mourn,
Swept on the surge of lines we speak and feel.

[Darkening Water]

Poe's Tomb

Stéphane Mallarmé

As into Himself at last Eternity
Changes him, the Poet with naked steel
Challenges an age afraid to feel
How that strange voice proclaims Death's victory!

They, with a hydra's twitch hearing the angel
Distill their *patois* to a purer sense,
Loudly denounce it witchcraft, drunk in the dense
Black brew of some dishonored spell.

From the hostile sky and earth, O grief!
If to adorn the dazzling tomb of Poe
Imagination carves no bas-relief

May this granite, from unknown disaster
Fallen here, at least its boundary show
To Blasphemy's black flights hereafter.

Crossing Walt Whitman Bridge

Walt, my old classmates who write poems
Have written poems to you.
They find you, old fruit,

In the supermarket, California;
They hear you speaking from the brazen mouth
Of your statue on Bear Mountain

In poems, so many poems—
You are large, you can contain them.
From my Philadelphia suburb I drive across

Walt Whitman Bridge
Into the freedom of New Jersey,
Passing the Walt Whitman Bar & Grill,

Walt Whitman Auto Parts & Junk Yard, Whitman
Theatre, Whitman Motor Inn,
Your Pharmacy, your Package Store,

Your Body Shop,
And yes,
Your supermarket's really in New Jersey!

Past old bottles, fenders, corrugated shacks,
Your neon name on mirrored doors
And winos slumped across the stoops

Shadowed by the boarded thirteen-storey
Walt Whitman Hotel no longer glutted
With Americans who'd never read a line of yours,

Speeding now, I think of you
Ingesting science, scent of haybarns, daily news and country bunkum
To translate the Farmer's Almanac into a Jeremiad

And mix the sinner's Presbyterian dreams into your cockalorum
(You Nosey Parker, peeping through the transom
Of his relentless dream),

To make the murmuration of crowds
Into leaves of compassion—
What you spit out

Would keep all Europe
Civilized two thousand years!
What have you left but

A larger continent
Bulging to belch and yawp, lusting
For the nightwind's breast, the curled

Lascivious kisses
Of the frondy sea? Approaching
Mannahatta (it waits

Where the road dips far ahead
Beyond the toll-booths and the tunnel,
Spires rising to jostle the horizon

Over fumes and loud arrivals,
The press of crowds as in the old days)
I think of you—prodigious

Your digestion, swallowing
Democracy, not flinching from the secret
Shame exposed by torchlit nightmare,

The drowned swimmer and the battle-death—
All the heroes! Pocahontas too!
A letch for handsome draymen,

Ecstasy in capillaries
As in turning stars—How did you
Rise through itches from the bed

You and your idiot brother
Shared in a drunken
Father's house, your flabby body

Indolently moving
Toward the lightning's revelation,
Fecundity sanspareil!

It wasn't easier before the advent
Of a landscape gouged for money
Or the coming down of fallout

Than now after the dismantling
Of the brave *Bonhomme Richard*
And the end of horsecars

To plant your seed
In Death's eyesocket
There to sprout in

Visionary life,
Always resurgent,
Never held down for long,

Felt alive,
Conceived and spoken,
So made true.

[Hang-Gliding from Helicon]

Snatches for Charles Ives

All those long dead New England farm boys
Sprang unarmed from R. W. Emerson's brain.
Where they fell they since have lain,
We forgot them like an old song out of mind,

Forgot their succor by the roadside spring,
Their probities before an angry God.
That upright Judge they judged them by is gone.
And who recalls the beehive hymnal drone

Uplifted souls made as they made concord?
What joy they found who found joy in the Word!
What martial airs were theirs, the fifetune boy's
Calliope that piped them, gay in blue

Files toward those backgrounds of ripped trees
And shattered waggons we've seen in Brady's
Photographs . . . They lie there where they've fallen,
All tent fires out, all camaraderies forgotten.

Torchlight parades! Magnetic energy of crowds!
Temperance and Tippecanoe! All those causes
Lost for long, dwindling with memory's losses,
Restored by these wild chords and sweet discords.

[Broken Laws]

Mark Twain, 1909

. . . his hair an aureole, white
cloud around a face half
eclipsed in shadow—*"Every one*
is a moon, and has a dark
side he never shows
to anybody"—in his white
suit, Palm Beach white, white
cravat, the eyes like cinders
gazing on devastation
past Mr. Amy crouched
beneath his black sheet, peering
toward the future. Behind him,
in the bookcase, only one
title in focus, thick book:
THE NILE. Always rivers,
rivers, the mind afloat on
currents, eddies . . . Memory
the raft that bears us onward,
onward, back to our threatened
Paradise, the waters
rising, where sounds of evening
—hoot owl, a barking dog—
are harbingers of death. It's
death that makes the present
ache so for the past, as
time that won't be stilled
swirls us toward an end we
cannot grasp. Like shadows
our story lengthens, lengthens
behind us. As Amy squeezes
the bulb, from the next room
—*"Youth!"*—Livy calls, he
starts, and this sitting
for the photograph is ended.

[Hang-Gliding from Helicon]

Concordance

AND his dark secret love
O rose, thou ART sick!
Has found out thy BED

Of CRIMSON joy
And his DARK secret love
Does thy life DESTROY

DOES thy life destroy
That FLIES in the night
Has FOUND out thy bed

HAS found out thy bed
And HIS dark secret love
On the HOWLING storm

That flies IN the night
IN the howling storm
The INVISIBLE worm

Of crimson JOY
Does thy LIFE destroy
And his dark secret LOVE

That flies in the NIGHT
O rose, thou art sick!
OF crimson joy

Has found OUT thy bed
O ROSE, thou art sick!
And his dark SECRET love

O rose, thou art SICK!
In the howling STORM
THAT flies in the night

THE invisible worm
That flies in THE night
In THE howling storm

O rose, THOU art sick!
Has found out THY bed
Does THY life destroy

The invisible WORM

Instructions to a Medium, to be transmitted to the shade of W. B. Yeats, the latter having responded in a séance held on 13 June 1965, its hundredth birthday:

You were wrong about the way it happens,
You, unwinding your long hank of that old yarn
    Spun from our common dream since chaos first receded,
    As though a superannuated Druid were needed.

What looms now on that desert where the birds
Turn in their frenzy and scream uncomprehending?
    Not a cradled beast in whom divinity
    Could repossess the earth with fierce majesty;

We've seen the coming of a dispensation
Miniaturized in our set on the tabletop:
    Blazing from its pad, that rigid rocket
    No larger than the ballpoint pencil in my pocket

With its sophisticated systems for manoeuvre
And retrieval, the bloated astronauts within
    Plugged to cardiometers in weightless flight
    —Their radiant spirals crease our outer night.

No, you were wrong about the way it happens.
Our radar scorns all horoscopes. Where Phaedrus
    Tumbling past perfection fell toward birth,
    Junked satellites in orbit ring the earth

And circuitry has made the Tetragrammaton
As obsolescent as a daft diviner's rod.
    Yet you, a boy, knelt under Knocknarea
    Where the cragged mountain buffeted the sea

And knew a cave beside that desolate shore
Had been the gate through which Christ harrowed Hell.
    But what could knowledge of that sort be worth?
    Imagination would not rest; from that day forth

God-driven, you toiled through our long-darkening age
To do the work the gods require. In love, in rage,
    You wrote no verse but glorifies the soul.
    What's history, that we should be imprisoned

By some contention of the passing minute,
No sooner won than lost by those who win it?
    All action's but a strut between the wings.
    Our part you knew we each must play by heart,

By heart-mysteries that no invention changes
Though knowledge further than our wisdom ranges.
    "What matter though numb nightmare ride on top?"
    You knew there'd be a perturbation in the skies,

You knew, whatever fearful turn would come
By our contrivance, or immortal from the womb,
    Violence must break old tables of the law
    And old solemnities toward desecration draw,

But how conceive coherence with our power?
Old ghost, you seem to beckon from your tower—
    Moon-magic is the grammar of your speech,
    A cast of thought to keep within our reach

The tragic gaiety of the hero's heart
That blazes where the soul consumes in art
    All reality as faggots for its fire,
    Revealing the desired in the desire.

Then man, though prisoned in his mortal day,
In imagination dominates all time,
    Creates that past and future between which his way
    Unwinds with the fated freedom of a rhyme.

[Striking the Stones]

Her Obedient Servant

Robert Graves, 1895–1985

He ferreted first things to their first cause:
The Alphabet, to trees in a Sacred Grove;
The one true theme of poetry, to love
Under the immitigable Muse's laws,

Her laws all else is lost for if obeyed,
Ardor inseparable from primal fright
As when bombardment raked his trench all night
And Reason gibbered in a world gone mad.

His gift was twinned, as he himself was twain—
His suppliant lover's, his strict captain's art
Found bliss and death clutched one to the other's heart,
For simple Truth with Paradox had lain.

His poems, spurning the chaos of our days,
On passion shed their coruscating blaze
As, at the instant of the year's ascension,
Stonehenge's heelstone pours the blinding sun.

[Hang-Gliding from Helicon]

Words for Dr. Williams

Wouldst thou grace this land with song?
    Well, go yodel your head off.
But if it's poems you want, then take a town
    with mills and chimneys, oil
Slithering on the river toward the falls,
    grit in the air, a man
Just off the night shift turning, tired yet strong
    to watch the girl who hurries
Toward a timeclock step down from the bus—
    slim ankles, one,
Two, and click click click swings past. The sun
    glints on her raincoat. There's
Your muse and hero. Stick around this town
    where people speak American
And love is possible—Your stethoscope
    held to our arteries
In sickness and in health you found some places
    where our own poems grow.

[Striking the Stones]

The Translators' Party

The great Polish
Emigré towered
Over the American
Poets at the party
For the contributors
Who'd wrested and wrought
The intractable consonants
Of Mickiewicz
Into a sort
Of approximate English,

Till Auden went over
To Jan Lechon,
Half a foot taller
Than the rest of us scribblers
And would-be reviewers,
Those venerables
For an hour reliving
A continent's culture,
Aperçus in the lilting
Accents heard

In cafés in Warsaw,
Vienna, Kracow . . .
One with the fiction
Of civilized discourse
In his native diction
Still entertainable
In imagination,
The other among
Aliens, aliens
In an alien tongue

For whom the greatness
Of the poet Adam
Mickiewicz can only
Be indirectly
Expounded, like Chopin's
Shown in slide-lectures

To a hall of wearers
Of battery-powered
Audiophones,
For whom his own poems

Cannot be known but
In deaf-and-dumb hand-signs,
No shades of his sounds, his passionate
Rhythms twisted.
His poems are stateless.
Yet it's Lechon's laughter
That I remember,
With one who could summon
A world lost in common
For an hour's reversal

Of an age's disaster
—Never known
To us in our *Times*
A fortnight after
Who read he was found
"Apparently fallen"
From his high window,
That voice
Stilled now
On New York's alien ground.

[The Center of Attention]

A Letter to W. H. Auden

Swarthmore, Pennsylvania

When the Romantic Ego had begun to fester
In the junkyard of its own corroded trophies
   —Shattered discs of Traubel in *The Ring,*
   Guns as obsolescent as the dragon,
     And piles of gold
Hoarded from teeth once filled by dentists in Berlin—

Some of us followed *maquis* in the liberation
Of the line from meters; other columns fought
   For freedom from dictatorships of logic
   Or purged their poems of lust for country lanes.
     But none prevailed
As did the Seeker in the land that never rains

Where our each loveless woe has been foretold and quoted
And footnoted, while bells toll on empty pews. That's how
   It was, when you came from your distant home,
   Abandoned mineshafts, rivers flowing North,
     And ancient rhythms
On the tongue. Across the border you stepped forth

From the nursery to schoolboy games, already
Armed with tricks and spells enough to stand the hairdos
   Of our Enemies on end. There, sly
   Error, in a fashionable skin
     —Already splitting—
Becomes a newer creature even as the eye

Takes in its forms, and by its form is taken in.
But none of Error's writhing heads knows what defences
   Could hold at bay the Hero of that Quest
   Whose end is with the honest Truth's reflection
     To jest and dazzle,
Then, with wit's quick strokes, lop off each one. Correction:

You made the near-perfection of your art reproach
For its botched work the slothful heart, under-achiever.
　　　Just down the street from my house stands the mock-
　　　Venetian villa with its tower, where
　　　　　You parsed and graded
Laborious compositions by the Chinese Air

Cadets and explications by indigenous
Co-eds whose children read you in my seminars.
　　　There you found a tongue for Caliban,
　　　There wrote of villagers who wouldn't see
　　　　　The unicorn
In their azaleas—yet still speak of that Englishman

Who shuffled in to dinner at the Ingleneuk
His feet in carpet slippers!—But of course you knew
　　　How Life, *l'homme moyen sensuel,* recalls
　　　The grace of vision as oddness of dress.
　　　　　For "Poetry
Makes nothing happen"—that is, nothing more, or less,

Than how we see reality. Now how we act,
That's our affair, not Poetry's; no use to hold
　　　The poem responsible for what the reader
　　　To whom its home truths bring the invitation,
　　　　　Change your life!
Does with his life. Enough, that in the ordination

Of your language—alliteration, zeugma, trope—
The blade of rectitude is sheathed in our delight.
　　　Those forms of feeling breathing in the forms
　　　Of verse resuscitate, in these dark days,
　　　　　Us who receive
Your gifts and offer you our gratitude, our praise.

[Hang-Gliding from Helicon]

The Sonnet

Remembering Louise Bogan

The Sonnet, she told the crowd of bearded
    youths, their hands exploring
       rumpled girls,
       is a sacred

vessel: it takes a civilization
       to conceive its shape or know
       its uses. The kids
       stared as though

a Sphinx now spake the riddle of
    a blasted day. And few,
       she said, who would
       be *avant-garde*

consider that the term is drawn
       from tactics in the Prussian
       war, nor think
       when once they've breached

the fortress of a form, then send
       their shock troops yet again
       to breach the form,
       there's no form—

. . . they asked for her opinion of
       "the poetry of Rock."
       After a drink
       with the professors

she said, This is a bad time,
       bad, for poetry.
       Then with maenad
       gaze upon

the imaged ghost of a comelier day:
    I've enjoyed this visit,
        your wife's sheets
        are Irish linen.

[*The Center of Attention*]

Delusions

Remembering John Berryman

If a genius committed his genius
To tunes the time's out of joint with—
Say, a sinfonietta for nose-flute
And three trombones;

Or choreographed on cobblestones
Pas de deux; or, beholding the end of an epoch,
This troubadour *would* make the point with
The Great American Epic

In a gab of which he's the sole speaker,
Scored for laughs and for moans
—A performance he won't make a dime with;
Though near perfect, what use to the seeker

Of perfections the joint's out of time with?
His lay he lays down by the mistress,
Heart's Ease, whose embraces he longs for,
His codpiece swelling, hopeless,

Driven daft by the muse he makes songs for.

[The Center of Attention]

Lines for Jack Clemo

author of *The Map of Clay,*
now blind and deaf,
a "Prisoner of God"

I stand on gritty Goonamarris,
The four elements assail me.
How can my senses hold all Nature's
Clarity and the soil of man?

He, leonine before the firescreen, paces
The kingdom of deprivation's borders
Striking the stones to make them sing.
No land's so bleak he cannot find those stones:

His Adversary guards the glazed ground.
They wrestle head to head and wound to wound,
Then inward darkness burns away,
Shards of silence frame the essential psalm.

[Striking the Stones]

High Society

"Toby's" in Cos Cob—faded mirrors, a smoked-wood bar
in an old roadhouse behind a row of trees,
still trading on the great ill fame
of those police raids years before.
Early, I sit at the table nearest the bandstand.
"Hey kid, better not let nobody
see ya drink that drink"—a great white
toothy smile, bulk of body heaving
in genial laughter, "or you'll spend
the night in jail," and the drummer tries
brushes on his snare. Cozy Cole
has talked to me! Now Art
Hodes puts his drink down carefully
in a coaster on the piano top and spreads
his left hand clear across a tenth, a twelfth,
riffles off some chords, as Max Kaminsky
—I'm a lot taller than he is—takes his seat,
warming the mouthpiece in one hand, the other
fingering the keys. Edmund Hall unpacks
his clarinet, fits the halves together, turns
the ridged nuts tightening his reed, then forms
his embouchure around the mouthpiece,
puts down the instrument and looks around,
sees me, transfixed to hear him play.
"Hiya kid, wasn't you at Nick's last Sat'day night?"
He remembers! Maybe he remembers
my telling him I'm trying to learn to play
like him . . . "Listen, kid,
before we start" (the somber room is still,
nearly empty under glum electric gaslamps)
"Lemme show you what you gotta know
if you're gonna play like me. D'ja ever
hear the Picou Chorus?" And now my heart's
a leaden fishweight. All those hours
replaying stacks of records bought
from the jukebox depot for a quarter each
(school lunch skimped for weeks to save the quarters),
my hoard of Bluebirds, red Vocallions, scratched Okehs,
discards from ginmills up and down the Post Road,

and I never heard the Picou Chorus
so look a dummy, knowing nothing, to Ed Hall.
"Yeah, old Alphonse Picou's chorus
in 'High Society' like I learned it
off Leon Rapallo who played it just
like old Alphonse Picou—He'd always play it,
even after he went off his nut
he'd play it all alone there in the bughouse
in N'Orleans. Somebody wants to play the clarinet
in N'Orleans, he's got to play that chorus. At your age
I could do it pretty good. It goes
like this—"
                    Ed Hall raises his clarinet and bursts
into a wailing skipped descent of sound
and the empty saloon in Connecticut
blacks out—in a whorehouse on a riverboat
in Storeyville the grace notes tumble like a ball of glass
bouncing down a marble staircase, sharp and cracking
but not breaking quite. Filling the spaces
between his note-stream and the silence,
sizzle-sizzle-sizzle and a tump-a-tump-a
as bass and snare pace out the shifting rhythms
and now come piano chords like pilings running
out on the river beneath a pier that holds
a palace, and Kaminsky's
trumpet obligato, muted, open,
muted, weaves the pendant pattern
of its chandeliers of sound while Edmund Hall
is leaping upward, bouncing back up up those gleaming
stairwells higher, till his slurred vibrato's
whipping down the blues arpeggio
to a clear, humming lower register so pure
it would melt the forged iron padlocks on the heart
of the attendant at Louisiana State
Hospital where Leon Rapallo,
brain gouged by syphilis, still plays
this chorus through the barred window
as the music floats off in a swirl
of motes dropping across a dusty road.
They run through "High Society" together, each
takes a riff in turn, bold flags
of different colors spearing off

from the onward repetition of the tune,
the tune ever changing as the jam-
session opens out in all directions
till they come back
acknowledging the single tune they
sprang from, now spring out anew, in different
riffs, new sharps, new blue notes, new returns,
by some invisible bond unspoken each attuned
to the knowledge that this chorus
is stop-and-go and hence the next-to-last
before the separate wills of clarinet and brasses
—Teagarden has joined them in the midst
of all of it and launched his sliding rough
caress of sound, his tiger's love-call romping
in the cellar under sweet suspended chords and
snaffled snares and rimshots' intuitions—all
coasting through the final chorus
of "High Society" and they reach
The End
                              They take a break,

laughing, wave to the applause of couples who've arrived
in Cords and rumbleseated roadsters,
youths in ice-cream flannels, yacht-club blazers, arms
around their silky girls with the white throats and low-cut dresses,
thin wrists, the ivory cigarette-holders drooping
from long fingers, already
smashed, still in the Flaming Twenties
like the music, though it's September,
1939, and few
of us will likely make
such insouciant, plangent joy as this
in the Forties or, if we get there,
in our forties although we spend
ourselves long times from now, trying
to remember
how it was, the Picou Chorus
and the other choruses
on shining instruments that plunge
against silence, quickening
in the illusion of their absolute
freedom the yoke of only four

chords and sixteen bars, borne
so gaily by Ed Hall,
Art Hodes, Cozy Cole, Max
And Jackson T. playing our hearts out,
each in his own way, together.

[Hang-Gliding from Helicon]

VIII

Summer

This busy day has poured on the horizon
A molten sky that cools,
Crystallizing into stars.

And these rocks with their smooth breasts,
Their dark mouths, exhale a fading
Warmth hoarded from memory of the sun.

A breeze tentatively comes from somewhere
Far at sea, searching for a lover,
For bestowal, bringing its caresses,

Bringing words etched on this page,
A white prow I launch now
To cleave the darkening water.

[Darkening Water]

A New Birth

While I turned in a warm cocoon
Man and Rome fell.
Furrows scarred the valleys.
Haggle, blow and toil
Echoed at the stony gates,
Yet discipleship to the seasons
Made gay the festival.

All that long labor made me
Who split my earthling skin
In a fallen wind, a dusty sky.
What patrimony I come by
Lies, an empty sack,
Shrivelled fables at my back.
This is a new birth I begin.

[The City of Satisfactions]

Treasure

Buried gold of my inmost distress
—Will it be always hid from me? I hold

Between my palms a forked divining rod,
And as I trudge on littered roads

Through the countries of one day
And another day, past empty houses,

Their abandoned banquets gnawed by mice
Where the musicians left without their pay,

The lovers vanished, the children gone,
The wise branch in my hands points down

Toward bulging sacks deep underground
Swelling with plenty, each night richer

Than before. Here's ransom for the king
Of the final country—he'll set free

The captive trumpeters, the missing lovers,
Children banished from their playthings,

And all lost years will be redeemed.

[Darkening Water]

A Visitation

Now why would a visitation from the Isles
Of the Blessèd come to Swarthmore,
PA 19081, a borough zoned
For single-family occupancy? No
Rocks of Renunciation on our
Assessors' rolls. Somewhere,
A consecrated shore
Ringed by dolmens where the wind speaks.
I listen to the hunger of the owl
Enclose the chipmunk in the quavering night,
I hear the plantain stretch its leaves to smother
Grass-shoots reaching toward the light.
The thick obituary of a lost day
Lies still on our writhing lawn.
And now the sky, black widow, pales
At the arrival of her new lover.
Between the thighs of trees old graves of sorrows
Open, and a fresh wind stirs.

[Striking the Stones]

In the Pitch of Night

White-throat beyond my window,
The sliver of your song
Pierces
The mist before the morning light
Shrivels the promises of night.

Your song
Changes nothing. The cold bay
Heaves and settles as before.
I cannot see you
In your cloudy tree.

Why do you thrust your silver knife
Into my silences? What undelivered
Letter will you open
Slitting the folded edges
Of my sleep?

It is darker
Before my open eyelids
Than in the clarity before
When I was hearing
From a burning tree

A sparrow sing.
I could all but see him in the blaze.
His unappeasable desire
Threaded across the sky
A testament of change,

Melting into song
Those pure resonances only
That echo
Without cease
Through discords dying all the day.

[Striking the Stones]

A Comfort

Where preening bottleflies endure
the heat without breathing and dust accepts
the prints of lizards' hands,

the sky stretches and melts,
and there's no shady grove beside
the clapboard farmhouse, unmended fence,

thin chickens squatting in its meager
veranda's shade—Won't you have a dipper
of this birch beer? I've just put a chunk of ice in—

taste of homebrew still remembered,
skinny freckled hands and yellow flowers
fading on an apron, her gaunt smile

a comfort remembered still
years and years
after she squanched the burning of the day.

Devotion

To carve this long-haired, melon-breasted girl,
His blade caressing every curve and curl
Of her slim hips and coiled, voluptuous tail,
Her lover had to slay, then flay, a whale.

[Darkening Water]

Literature

We, when young, had a professor
Who, between our immature
Selves and poems, was intercessor.
So we learned of love; and of literature,

How even a single image wrests
From oblivion its maker's name.
But who, then, wrote his mistress's breasts
Were strawberries floating on the cream?

In the Graeco-Roman Room

I have seen 21 beautiful and naked
Aphrodites, each one arching
Her small right foot, her slender
Arms clasping the shift of wind
Against her breasts. One can desire
What may scarcely be believed in,

One can admire the dozen Hercules
And Herakleses, archaic heroes
Of the unprotected private parts,
So strong the skins of their
Flayed lions seem
To grow from their own shoulders

—these, the idols of an Age of Error.
Not to be said though of the bronze
mouse $1^1/_4$
inches high blowing
a trumpet, one small paw and elbow
stopping his own ears.

[Broken Laws]

First Flight

I watches me climb
in the cockpit, him fixing
the belt and waving
my hand I see

the prop rev and the plane
cough forward
both wings biting
sudden wind

I on ground invisible
sees me taxi obvious
behind him Wild Pilot
what I doing there & here

particularly when
up high he says
Dan,
he says, Dan boy,

take over I don't feel
too good after all
that Scotch-type rot
last night I'm flying

me at the joystick o
boy how come
those chickens getting bigger chasing
their shadows under stoops

I see it clearly
clearly
STICK BACK!
and we climb

higher than the sun
sinking in a stew of clouds
Well Major anything
for a laugh me say

I say let's bring her down

[Striking the Stones]

The Finish

The first runner reached us
bearing the news before
he was expected by
the camera crew—the instant
replay showed him standing
by the roadside, sucking
half an orange. Who'd think
he had endured so many
miles? They demanded
he re-run the final
fifty yards while they
re-filmed him. While they filmed him
a second runner crossed
the line but by the time
the cameras turned to him
the second runner wasn't
running any longer
but sucking half an orange;
he too must re-enact
the second finish, since
the public is entitled
to the real thing.
Just as he re-crossed
the line, finishing second
a second time, here comes
puffing up the hill
the third man, at his heels
the crazy crowd the first
runner came to tell of
but had no chance to tell
anyone while cameras
caught his second first
finish and then turned
from him and scanned the second
finish of the second
finisher, the spent
third man with an orange
in his hand, the raggle-
taggle mob arriving

at the reviewing stand
and soon there's blood all over
the finish line and no
reviewers and no stand,
but what viewer could believe
this, cameras still
following the third
man suck his orange? The crews
urge the crowd once more
to re-enact the finish—

Saturday

An experiment results in the transmutation
    of a fly and a man. When
the old castle of a vampire baron is restored
    the baron returns and goes
on a killing spree. A mad scientist transplants his
    insane assistant's brain in
another human. After a baby sea-monster
    is captured off the coast of
Ireland and placed in a London circus, its angry
    father makes a shambles of
the city. Suffering from exhaustion, a pop singer
    comes to a bee farm for rest
only to find her life endangered by the insane
    beekeeper. A vampire must
prey upon living humans to sustain its own life.
    The life of a young woman
is irrevocably changed when she moves into a
    sinister house. A public
opinion analyst, stumbling on a hillbilly
    family, becomes involved
in murder. A successful songwriter decides to
    pursue the girl of his dreams.

[Darkening Water]

Owed to Dejection

The way the one who O so narrowly
won the election
bestows dejection

upon the one who O so nearly
won, the election
leaves him as a suitor

about to elope is left
with reservations for a double
and no hope

in his new role
as unloved lover
with no other

career opening,
yet in dreams, determined,
ardent, still he woos her

though she turn her face
from his embrace
as adamant in rejection

as the crowd
that spurns the loser
of an election.

Breathing Purely

Now, at last,
I carry nothing
In my briefcase
And an empty mind.
In the meadow

Under the chestnut tree
I am a part of what I see.
Swallows above the alder thicket
Skim mosquitoes from the haze,
And I've seceded

From all committees, left
My Letters to the Editor unsent
No solutions, no opinions.
Breathing purely
Without ambitions, purged, awaiting

Annunciations of the true.
The wind is up now and the swallows gone.
I'll listen to the chestnut tree
Rustling
Empty-headed in the wind.

[Striking the Stones]

At Evening

At evening comes a certain hour
When the teeming world remembers
It is a hostage of the dead.

Then bend in homage
The tall trees whose sprinkle of seeds
Tickled the wind. The wind is dying.

This is the hour when dust
Gleams as the tired corona leans
Its bloodied head against the rim of sky

And the dark night girds
Beyond the pulsing stars
To drop its pomps of mourning down.

From windows of the houses come
Colloquial sounds and pungent odors,
Alien rhythms thrust against the night.

[Striking the Stones]

Going

Your time has come, the yellowed
light of the weary sun
wavers in the foliage.
It's no use, no use to linger.
So, goodbye, day. See,
the shadows join each other
as the air turns shadow
and the light fails. You
are gone, gone into the ghostly
light of all my days, of all
my hungers only partially assuaged,
of all desires
which in the rush of hours
I reached and stooped to grasp.
They're gone, receding like the light,
like the shadows, receding
into subsidence, to come
again as day comes,
as the night
comes, bringing its own
going in its coming
again, and again.

[Darkening Water]

Who We Are

On a morning like this one, when the mist is lit from within,
a silvery light without center that envelops you so that you breathe
light in the air and you can't even see to the mailbox, it's then
you feel cut off from time, dangling in space suspended: Where
in this silvery glow are the deeds, the chants, the annals, the tales
of the Founders of Cities, the Heroes who saved us from past
allegorical monsters, historical perils, from real dangers imagined
and imaginary dangers made real by being
predicted after the fact by poet and oracle? It was
these—the strophes that told how Grandfather's own great-grandfather,
with only his own shrewd courage and motherwit, broke
the back of the wind and manacled wrists of the waves,
by guise and disguise outwitting the one-eyed warrior-shaman
who led the horde that surrounded our palisade (Remember
how his captive Raven leapt on the enemy's head, black
wings blindfolding the chieftain's eye while the great beak croaked
its doomward prophecy, routing
all terrified outlanders!)—it was these,
as we coped each day with a new raw dawn, a further
spilling of the sun in the roiling sea, that made us aware
of who we are and in that knowing
felt resurgent the ancient strengths of night and early day. Nothing
there was in our world that denied us this: The brickwork city,
the wooden sills, the clay rooftiles, the gables, steeples, the pewter
mugs, stoneware jugs, the cobbled streets, toward evening
the reaching shadows, all, all were what they were, none threatened
the clock with a sundial's obsolescence where the garden fountain
is perpetually lit by light that has no need to heed
where our tiny sun and insignificant speck of moon may chance
to float in their cubit of space around this dustfleck
we do our dreams on. Now, if we could see
through the globuled light like a featureless movie screen
with only the projector's bulb intensified before the flicker
of coming attractions disturbs and distorts the blazing white
monochrome of its purity, we could find
what denies us this. Denies
by the hum and clatter that rise not with the wind nor fall as the wind fades,
denies by the clutter of junked vehicles encircling earth in rings
parodic of those other planets' moons, denies by thrusting, swollen shadow

of mushroom clouds that billow above the wind and drop their wizard's curses
on distant pasturage, on heads of newborn babes. Denies
the place of our space, denies the time
of our time gone before, expanse of time
stretching as a prairie on which the first covered wagon had but travelled
the first few leagues while ahead there beckoned
undulant plain, the rumbling bison herds, a vivid sky
streaked with circling hawk and eagle, now shrunken out of mind
behind the gilded arches of our miracle miles, our
car lots, parking lots, developed lots, the neon arms
arching over asphalt so that night shall never fall.
The fourteen screens in the show window all are tuned
to the same minuscule mannikin in unison enacting
the same holdup firing the same shot driving the getaway car in wild evasion
of the same pursuit crashing the same barrier amid the same
crescendo of squealing tires and the same
interruptions announcing the virtues of the same
floor cleaner. Now
will your lines recall
our vanished world as far behind us now as
Achilles' vengeance was and the heaped dead and blackened stumps
of Troy's walls fallen in twilight were to those Achaean towns
that required a blind man's lyre to keep them from forgetting,
or will your lines take shape from the shapelessness around you,
the jointed facts devoid of nature where our hive
pursues and still pursues our ends
unknown while stars still hold their posts in beleaguered constellations,
and still the planets swing in accustomed arcs around us, and the earth
ignorant of our quick profits and brief pleasures, as before
drinks rain, hoards its green force through seasons of ice, of deprivation,
till it feed roots again, offers its annual bounty to the fecund, the lucky
fields of daisies, the woodchuck in the bank, the treetop cicada
who, living in time's terrain and in the rhythms
of space, of space and time know nothing.

[Darkening Water]

Called Back

It's got to be a big one, so resonant
is its repeated cry—the sound of a cracked
bronze bell twice struck under water
—so it's not a bittern ("a slow, deep
ong-ka-choonk, ong-ka-choonk"), nor a Great
Blue Heron ("Deep harsh croaks: *frahnk, frahnk,
frahnk*") that keeps on throbbing in the twilight,
in deepening dark, till, in thick woods, sounding
closer now, the insistent, endlessly
repeated call—through the fringe of tall spruce
at the field's edge I with fox-tread walk, thrust
onward toward the bird's reclusive summons,
seeming nearer, by black boughs concealed now,
then farther off, in deeper, darker woods,
so I press through the warm and moist black air
at once so menacing, yet half-familiar
as though, sometime, before remembering,
I'd been here and the two-toned urgent throbbing
in my ears, my arms, my chest, was all
that I could hear in all-encroaching blackness
till from that impenetrable murk I burst
free, in a clearing, rock-crags under sky!
I climb the cairn at the center of this field
at the center of the forest—there, above
Orion's shoulders, the whole vast turning sky
alight with planets, constellations, stars,
a silky wash of dots banding the heavens
where, as I watch, light from the faintest,
farthest sources mingles with the flecks
from nearer stars, and closer still the sudden
streaking meteors, the Perseids showering
lines of light that fade as soon as seen,
—Time made visible as space, contained
in my stunned gaze that holds at once
the end and the beginning and the black
blankness of the unlit nothing that precedes
the first, the earliest, the oldest light.

[Darkening Water]

A Witness

When asked by Friends to speak of poetry
what could I say?
It did seem preordained
in the only house of worship in the Commonwealth
named for a poet, that I read
Winfield Scott's noble colloquial poem,
"It is easier to forget than to have been
Mr. Whittier . . ." How different
from the homely rhetoric of Whittier,
yet probity of discourse as of purpose
and the feeling so much finer
than any of the words.
Quakers, in song, sing Whittier's words,
praying, wring the tongue with silence—
no words, or few.
In the spare meetinghouse
in the quietest beseeching,
the only ornament involuntary rainbows
where from a cracked pane wintry light
leapt, broken
colors vivid on a wall of white,
with heads bowed,
the world renounced as long as stillness
echoed in the room,
Friends prayed. We felt the silence
swell with concentrated purpose,
syllables of thought
in questioning, in waiting,
and the light shift
clearer a little.

[Darkening Water]

Notes

Poems, ideally, should contain within themselves all that their readers need to know. The passing of time, however, has eroded common knowledge of some things and persons mentioned in the poems for which I offer clarification below.

"In the Days of Rin-Tin-Tin": This poem is built on allusions to popular culture in the 1920s and 1930s.

"Rin-Tin-Tin": the heroic dog in Saturday morning serial films, 1930s.

"the deliquescent horn of Bix": Bix Beiderbecke, lyrical jazz cornettist, d. 1931.

"Ostrich walk," "Ja-da": popular 1920s dance step and jazz tune.

"Readily admitted the Victorian wrong" alludes to Lytton Strachey's popular debunking book *The Victorians* (1919).

"Caligari . . .": menacing character in the German expressionist film (1920), described as "a symbol of insane tyranny, and of the tendencies in Weimar Germany that would lead to Hitler and fascism"—Mike Budd, *The Cabinet of Dr. Caligari: Texts, Contexts, Histories* (Rutgers University Press, 1990), p. 1.

"the Little Fellow": Charlie Chaplin's self-designated nickname; also refers to the speaker of the poem.

"Flushing Meadows, 1939": site of the 1939 World's Fair.

"glimmering globe . . . spired hope . . .": The architectural logo of the Fair was a tall trylon and a huge globe.

"Crop-Dusting": method used by U.S. forces to destroy harvests of the Viet Cong.

"In Memory of Lewis Corey": Luigi Fraina helped found the Communist Party, USA, but was intellectually too independent to submit to party-line orthodoxy. In his new identity as Lewis Corey, he became an independent Marxist economist; author of *The Decline of American Capitalism* (1934) and other widely read books. While I was stationed at Wright Field, Ohio, in 1944–45, I met Corey, then a professor at Antioch College. For details, see my *Zone of the Interior*, pp. 90–97. "Archangel . . .": U.S. and British forces attempted to negate the Bolshevik Revolution by invading Archangel in 1920, a failed campaign.

"The Princess Casamassima": Like Henry James's princess, Catherine Wilkerson, my former student at Swarthmore College, joined a radical cause in the 1960s, the Weathermen. Several colleagues, making bombs in the basement of her father's house, blew themselves up. The house was formerly owned by James Merrill's family—see his poem "18 West 11th Street," in *Braving the Elements*. Cathy Wilkerson survived the bombing and disappeared; after ten years as a fugitive, she surrendered in 1980 and received a sentence of three years in prison for possession of dynamite.

"Rats": a folk remedy, heard many years ago from a neighbor on Cape Rosier, Maine.

"A Riddle": Peace.

"As I Was Going to Saint-Ives": A formerly well-known children's riddle:

> As I was going to Saint-Ives
> I met a man with seven wives.
> Each wife had seven sacks,
> Each sack had seven cats,
> Each cat had seven kits.
> Cats, kits, sacks, wives:
> How many were going to Saint-Ives?

I find this riddle has been quite displaced among the young by TV and other contemporary obliterators of traditional oral culture. St. Ives is the most westerly point of the British Isles; the west is traditionally associated with death, so a journey thither has the implication of moving toward life's end. In the poem, the speaker and the man he meets are both going to St. Ives.

"Lines for Scott Nearing": Scott Nearing, radical economist, author of *Living the Good Life* and other books of social commentary. Our neighbors on Cape Rosier, he and his wife grew their own food, renounced modern life, and for their self-sufficiency became, in the 1970s, icons to a generation of readers of *The Whole Earth Catalogue*. "Albania": Enver Hoxha, the Stalinist dictator, feted Nearing on his visits there.

"The Peaceable Kingdom": section III, "Barnard's pendant lightless star," discovered by the late Swarthmore astronomy professor Peter Van de Kamp.

"Poe's Tomb": my translation of "Au Tombeau d'Edgar Poe," sent by Stéphane Mallarmé to be read at the dedication of a monument in Baltimore commemorating the twenty-fifth anniversary of Poe's death in 1874.

"Mark Twain, 1909": *"Every man is a moon . . . ."*: "Pudd'nhead Wilson's New Calendar," epigraph to chapter LXVI, *Following the Equator*.